Independent Kenya

To All Those Who in Defiance Seek New Beginnings

Front Cover:
Hakuna Njia Hapa: Keep Out — Private Property
Cheche Kenya: The Voice of Kenya

Independent Kenya

Authors: The Kenyan authors of this book have to remain anonymous because they are still living in their country.

Sponsored by the Journal of African Marxists

In solidarity with the authors

Published by Zed Press

Independent Kenya was first published by Zed Press, 57
Caledonian Road, London N1 9DN in 1982, having been
sponsored by the Journal of African Marxists, P.O. Box 35579,
Lusaka, Zambia and 57 Caledonian Road, London N1 9DN,
United Kingdom — in solidarity with the authors.

Copyright © Journal of African Marxists on behalf of the
authors, 1982

Copyedited by Anna Gourlay
Proofread by Mark Gourlay and Devdan Sen
Cover Design by Jan Brown
Cover concept by the authors
Typeset by Jo Marsh
Printed in Great Britain

British Library Cataloguing in Publication Data

Independent Kenya
1. Kenya—History—1963-
967.6'204   DT433.580

ISBN 0-86232-078-X
ISBN 0-86232-079-8 Pbk

U.S. Distributor:
Lawrence Hill & Co., 520 Riverside Avenue, Westport,
Conn. 06880, U.S.A.

Contents

Abbreviations

COTU	Central Organization of Trade Unions
CPE	Certificate of Primary Education
DC	District Commissioner
DFCK	Development Finance Corporation of Kenya
DO	District Officer
EACE	East African Certificate of Education
GSU	General Service Unit
ICDC	Industrial and Commercial Development Corporation
ICFTU	International Confederation of Free Trade Unions
ILO	International Labour Office
IMF	International Monetary Fund
KADU	Kenya African Democratic Union
KANU	Kenya African National Union
KAU	Kenya African Union
KCC	Kenya Creameries Corporation
KKM	*Kiama kia Muingi*
KMC	Kenya Meat Corporation
KPCU	Kenya People's Cooperative Union
KPU	Kenya People's Union
KTDA	Kenya Tea Development Authority
PC	Provincial Commissioner

Glossary of Swahili Words

apana firiki mzungu tarekebish	don't worry, the white man will take care of it
askari	guard, soldier
asomi	those who read, the educated
aya(h)	children's nurse/'nanny'
chura	lavatory cleaner
giriminti	agree/with a contract
hakuna kazi	no work
hakuna njia hapa	no way through/private property
Harambee	get on with it!
jiko(s)	cooking place
kaburu	Boer/South African
Kiama kia Muingi (Kikuyu)	name of political party
kibarua	day-labourer
kutumbuzi raisi	praising the President
magendo	black-market
majimbo	administrative districts, decentralizatio
matatu	free-lance pick-ups/mammy-wagon
matunda ya uhuru	fruits of independence
mnyapara	overseer, exploiter
ntukufu Mzee	our glorious father
nyang'au	hyena, ogre (Kikuyu)
nyayo(ism)	footprints/conforming
payukaring	'gabbling' (spreading rumours/ talking rubbish)
rungu	club/knobkerrie
saida Maskini	help the poor (beggar's cry)
shamba	plot/garden
twelekeene	let's go!
uchawi	witchcraft
waBenzi	those with Mercedes-Benzs

Introduction

Nearly twenty years ago, we were nominally granted our independence. At the time we made certain assumptions, which in retrospect seem politically naive. We assumed that 'independence' would initiate a radical departure from colonial arrangements, a departure which would fully mobilize the energies of self-motivated and dedicated Kenyans. We believed that the end of colonialism would mean the beginning of an equitable and democratic development of our natural and human resources. We thought, in short, that 'independence' would be *real* for our country and its people, and that we would take collective responsibility to preserve and enhance it.

We can no longer afford to be naive. The intervening decades have demonstrated that 'independence' can in fact point the way to a deepening state of economic, political, and spiritual dependence. 'Independence' in Kenya has led to the looting and squandering of our resources, and the virtual silencing of our people. It has led to increasing misery and impoverishment for the many. Aspirations for better lives under *uhuru* have been betrayed by predatory politicians who talk of 'nation-building' while fattening on the nation's wealth and people's labour. The system which our so-called 'leaders' have created is used to deny us our basic democratic rights and keep us perpetually subordinate. We are informed that criticism will be treated as subversion, and that we have nothing to do but obey and follow where they lead. They lead us further along the path of dependence, debt and national decline.

The situation in which we find ourselves today is grim. It would, however, be more demoralizing if our rulers were completely successful in their attempts to render us passive and impotent. But there are a few signs that repressive official ideology — which seeks to deny us *any* participation in political life, except as followers or spectators — is not proving entirely effective. In rural and urban areas, Kenyans are beginning to see through official propaganda and awaken to a sense of their own true interests. Here and there, against considerable odds, people are coming together to discuss the current predicament in which we find ourselves and to seek possible routes of escape from it.

This study has been produced by a discussion group which has met over a lengthy period to investigate and debate issues of national interest. We decided to circulate our ideas in written form out of the conviction that it is our duty as patriotic Kenyans to alert our countrymen to their true condition, and encourage them to bring their own critical faculties into play. We hope to reach a wider audience than that usually interested in the debates of a purely academic community. Those among us who are academics have studied and digested scholarly arguments concerning neo-colonialism, and recent ideas on political and economic developments in Kenya. Others, in manual employment, have drawn on their own experiences. We have presented our findings assertively, as simple declarations. The condensed nature of this work is a result of the difficult circumstances under which it was produced, which made it impossible to carry out open investigations and produce a detailed presentation. All our statements, however, are either derived from first-hand experience or are documentable, but we have deliberately chosen a format exclusive of references and footnotes since our purpose is not a narrowly scholastic one.

Instead, our purpose is to clarify our situation as simply and directly as possible, in a way that will stimulate Kenyans to think for themselves and mobilize their own strength and capacity for action, as peoples who are struggling for their liberation are doing all over the world. We hope that, as our people move from individual recognition of their plight to organized resistance many more discussion groups will be formed and other studies undertaken. We admit that the stage of organized resistance is not at hand. Ground must be prepared for resistance, by debate at all levels of society, by arousing a new awareness and determination among our peoples, and by what can be called cultural and political ferment. We would obviously prefer to discuss issues of such vital importance to Kenya openly, but given the repressive nature of the regime such an approach is not possible now. The regime's refusal to tolerate *any* discussion or debate demonstrates its essential insecurity, and forces groups like ours to work covertly with all the pressure and limitations that involves. We must accept this situation and resolve to work within it. We must not be deterred by the danger and difficulty of associating together, for only by defying our rulers' attempts to divide and subdue us can we hope to create for ourselves a new sense of direction and the strength of purpose to follow it.

As a first step along the path to our long-delayed 'independence' we must take our bearings and find out where we are now. We must try to understand what has become of our country, and why. Only by honestly accepting our present circumstances can we work to transform them. This study grew out of the attempts of our group to confront the implications of our current predicament, and find for ourselves and our country a route to national survival and progress. We are fully aware that we must not expect to be 'led' along that route, but must each — as thinking, active and working individuals — contribute to chart the way forward. We have too often been 'led' in the past, and must now break the ties of dependency and rely on our individual and collective resources.

In so doing, we will see our situation in its proper perspective. For we have not been brought to our present impasse solely by this or that individual. The system which dominates and oppresses us is larger than the personalities who serve it. What we must actively oppose is the system, not simply any particular individual or even the entire ruling clique. In the future individuals will come and go, but the system will remain the same, or worse, unless we can look beyond personalities to the underlying realities which have denied us meaningful independence. Future politics must again deal with these realities — with *issues* — not merely with personalities. By recognizing the issues at stake, we will gradually be able to regain the singleness of purpose and the power we possessed when we took up arms against the system of colonialism, not merely against this or that colonial governor. That system has been perpetuated in 'independent' Kenya in a different guise. That system remains the enemy. We can only go forward if we are clear on this fact and prepared for sacrifice and united resistance.

1. Birth of Our Power: Should We Forget the Past?

History, for most of us, is something we have been taught in school about our past and place in the world. It comes to us out of tedious textbooks, generally written by foreigners. Most Kenyan historians have added little to our understanding of whom we are, tending to see our pre-colonial history as a series of aimless wanderings and endless genealogies. Their writings seem as aimless as the migrations which they set out to trace and leave us with a stunted understanding of our past.

Our history must properly be seen as a record of the efforts of our people to transform nature for their own use. Our societies were never static. Our peoples had contact — often extensive — with each other and with foreigners who visited our shores. Sometimes these contacts were violent, taking the form of warfare and raiding. More often, they were peaceful, with material conditions of existence being gradually modified by barter and negotiation between ethnic groups. Some groups were expanding in numbers and land use before the British arrived. Others, expecially the pastoral peoples, were in the mid- and late Nineteenth Century weakened by drought and disease. Until the advent of British colonialism our material base and level of productivity came up against *natural* barriers, such as insufficient rainfall for reliable agriculture and herding. After the British take-over, colonialism itself, not nature, frustrated our further development as a people. We were ruthlessly introduced to the capitalist mode of production by foreigners who plundered our resources and commandeered our labour. We were told what to grow and what not to grow, how and where to live. Our independence of action was taken from us.

That independence has never been regained. The past most clearly embedded in the Kenyan present is our colonial one. We see, in our supposedly independent land, the mass of our people creating wealth for others to steal. This situation is not unique to our country. However, the *extent* of foreign domination, as well as the way our present rulers imitate their colonial predecessors, distinguishes us as a neo-colony in its starkest sense.

Our continued dependence is a fact we face in all our social, political, and economic activities. Our paltry intellectual life reminds us that we have been mentally enslaved as well as physically colonized. Our sham independence perpetuates the forms, institutions, and aspirations that we inherited from our colonial rulers.

However, a glance at the past shows an important difference between colonial Kenya and the Kenya of today. In the colonial past it is true that we were dominated, but at the same time we actively made our own history through our resistance. At no point during the 60 years of direct colonial rule did our parents and grandparents passively submit to foreign domination. They generally managed to retain a clear idea of their true interests and the nature of the enemy.

In post-colonial Kenya that idea has been obscured. Our lying, self-interested 'leaders' have dispossessed us of the right to think for ourselves and to pass judgment on policies they make in our name. We are forbidden to challenge their interpretation of 'nation-building'. We have been denied a voice in the shaping of our country. Meanwhile, our leaders, essentially parasitic and unproductive, imitate and impersonate a productive capitalist ruling class. They behave as the natural successors of the colonial masters, in whose footsteps they follow, and willing collaborators with our present foreign economic overlords. They lie to us, saying that we are fortunate to have a stable government dedicated to its people's true interests. They then deprive us of the means of assessing our good fortune or lack of it for ourselves. We are unable to engage in independent political and intellectual activity in 'free' Kenya. The freedom to discuss, to transmit ideas and information, has been denied us. Our leaders force us into becoming a passive population, deprived of the initiative and the language we once possessed — a language with which we formerly voiced our refusal to go tamely along with the violation of our most basic interests and needs. We must rediscover for ourselves the language of protest, and the mental and organizational tools with which to clarify our situation. We must regain a proper perception of the direction in which our nation is moving in order once again to become *active* participants in our own history: to make it, and not merely be made by it.

What then, can we learn from our colonial history? What does it tell us which can help us understand and change the circumstances in which we find ourselves?

The Colonial Past

Our textbooks tell us that the British grabbed our land for our own good. They were out to eradicate the slave trade and spread a 'civilizing mission' designed to make of us full human beings, on earth and in heaven. Britain's actual motives in extending imperial rule over one-quarter of the world's surface were hardly charitable. In the closing decades of the Nineteenth Century Britain faced increasingly stiff competition from major European industrial powers for markets and sources of raw materials. No longer could she hope that the informal 'spheres of influence' which her navy had extended over parts of Africa's coasts would ward off rivals. Direct territorial take-over was a way of forestalling competition and controlling areas of strategic economic value.

Initially, the land which became Kenya was viewed by the imperialists as more of a nuisance than anything else. In British eyes it appeared as nothing more promising than a dreary stretch of hot, dry bush which had to be crossed to get to Uganda, the source of the head-waters of the Nile and seemingly boundless fertility and potential wealth. Lusting after Uganda, the British, in the closing years of the Nineteenth Century, gained access to it by building a railway across our land which they had declared a British Protectorate. After centuries of positive contacts and trade with foreigners in the Indian Ocean region, after prolonged encounters with Arabs searching for slaves, and Portuguese trying unsuccessfully to plant a colony along our coast, East Africans were assaulted by invaders who meant to stay. They meant to stay and make the peoples of what was soon called Kenya pay heavily for their presence.

The immediate preoccupation of the British was how to make the railway profitable. The solution, which they gradually stumbled upon, was to make the territory of Kenya a 'White Man's Country', where European settlers would take for themselves all the best agricultural land and produce something for the railway to transport. The massive land grab of what became known as the 'White Highlands' was forced upon reluctant or indecisive British officials

3

by rogue aristocrats, like Lord Delamere, who simply arrived, looked, and took what they wanted, leaving the administration to rationalize their activities in subsequent land policies.

The Settler Economy

There was nothing systematic and well-planned about the process which made Kenya a settler colony. By World War I a fixed policy on land alienation had still not been decided upon by the colonial government, but their dithering made little difference to the thousand or so Europeans and Boers — the *kaburus* — who decided to force the ineffectual administration to see matters their way.

A few, more far-sighted, officials argued that a settler-dominated economy would prove to be more trouble than it was worth. It could be both needlessly expensive and politically dangerous. There were other ways to exploit the colony, which entailed fewer risks and less effort on the part of the *colonists*. Whereas white farmers would demand access to a well-developed infrastructure, police force and a large mobile labour force, African peasants could be made to produce for the market with less fuss and disturbance, depending on their own household labour. African cash-crop production would minimize social disruption and the potential for political disaffection or resistance.

Such a commonsensical approach to colonial exploitation was not to be heeded. After World War I an over-populated Britain willingly exported its land-hungry citizens and rewarded its soldiers with land grants in Kenya. By the 1950s, when our people took up arms to reclaim their country, a mere 4,000 white settlers were in possession of over seven million acres of the best land in Kenya, only a tiny proportion of which was put to productive use. The settlers had made our country into their exclusive playground, and our people their slaves. They despised us and they needed us. They robbed us, murdered us, and told us we should be grateful for their coming, that we should be content to serve the 'master race' indefinitely, in what they called 'White Man's Country'.

Kenya as 'White Man's Country' contained glaring contradictions. Threatened by Asian competition, in 1923 the settlers grudgingly went along with the Devonshire White Paper, which put the Asians in their place by declaring that *African* interests were to be 'paramount'. This meant, of course, that African interests were to be dismissed out of hand: African economic competition, if allowed, would highlight the weakness of the settler position. Dependent on forced labour and tax revenue extracted from our people by a variety of ruthless measures, the settlers were essentially a pack of parasitic fortune-hunters, kept in business by cheap forced labour, expensive state subsidies and guaranteed high prices for their commodities. The colonial administration denied them what they were seeking — total self-government — but allowed them a more or less free hand in such amusements as using Africans for target practice and flogging workers to death. The government, meanwhile, created such monopoly economic structures as the Maize Marketing Board, to prop up settlers who were constantly on the verge of bankruptcy, and prevented Africans from growing cash-crops and developing rival marketing systems. Before World War II, Africans were expected to know and keep their place — at the bottom. Our grandparents were told by the missionaries that their proper role was one of industrious service, for several hundred years at least. Only then a few 'choice spirits' might emerge to stand beside the Europeans in the governance of our land. The loss of their land, independence, and way of life was, they were told, a small price to pay for the gift of 'civilization' and Christianity.

Thus, our people became prisoners in their own country. They were penned in 'reserves', the able-bodied among them forced by tax policy and unscrupulous chiefs to go and work for a pittance on mixed farms, plantations, and in towns; to be flung back into the 'reserves' when no longer needed. The family which remained behind was expected to scrape together its own subsistence from the small, exhausted patches of land, for the wage paid to the worker hardly enabled him to secure his own food. By World War II, nearly half the African paid work-force squatted in towns. An artificial colonial city like Nairobi, built to service the pleasures and needs of the white rulers, developed a shanty-town culture. As in South Africa today, our fathers and mothers were supposed to be *chura* and *ayas*, do the work and then disappear. They 'disappeared' into slum locations like Kibera, Pumwani, and Pangani where, together, they developed a political consciousness about their social and economic enslavement.

Meanwhile, the 'reserves' became increasingly overcrowded and infertile. 200,000 or so of our people had been forced to go to the Rift Valley in search of work on settler farms, and land on which they could squat with their families and livestock. In the 1940s, they were threatened with permanent homelessness when the whites ordered mass evictions of squatters. They were ordered to 'disappear' back into the 'reserves', and become 'invisible' until such time as they could again be put to profitable use by the colonial settlers. Most of them joined the growing numbers of the landless, and watched their living conditions deteriorate year by year. In the early 1950s Kenya's Africans earned a per capita income of only £3 a year. During the 1930s and 1940s the price of maizemeal had increased by 800%. Not only did colonialism fail to bring any 'development' to our people, who were looted of the proceeds of their labour and their land for the benefit of the foreign minority, it also increasingly deprived our people of the means to feed themselves. They were deemed an expendable population, one which should be bled dry in the service of Empire.

World War II and After

During World War II the blood of our fathers was spilled in the service of murderous Europeans. During the 1940s, nearly 100,000 of Kenya's five million inhabitants were pressed into the war. For many Africans who went abroad with the British army — men like Kaggia and Kimathi — the situation in which they found themselves was a profoundly radicalizing one. Our men saw the 'civilizing mission' in a new light. Behind European claims to be agents of a superior civilization they discovered a brutality and racist-inspired genocide beyond all imagining. They recognized for what it was the hypocrisy of the British, who claimed to be fighting German racism while treating their own subject peoples in a similar way — as sub-human species.

Our men fought and died for the British. The message that greeted them on their return was a simple one: nothing has changed, you are still merely servants in your own country. There were signs of worse to come. For the settlers had reached the peak of their domination during the war years, when they had a free hand to do as they liked as long as they supplied the armies with food. Their numbers were growing. 8,000 new white immigrants entered the colony after the war, hoping to settle in the 'White Highlands'. As far as European farmers were concerned, things had never looked more promising in 'White Man's Country'. They confidently expected it to last forever.

But other imperialists saw matters differently after the war. Britain had been devastated by the war. Her economy was in ruins, while that of the only combatant to escape war-damage — the U.S.A.

— was vigorous. Britain realized that she would have to cut her
losses and shed some of the expenses of maintaining an Empire.
She would have to modify her colonial policy in order to stimulate
her industry and improve her adverse balance of payments. After
the war, Britain encouraged her industries to invest in manufacturing
in the colonies, not merely to extract raw materials from them.
Capitalism, meanwhile, expanded rapidly under the dominance of
the United States. International capital, large banks and trading
companies moved into Nairobi, and transformed the city into a
regional financial, marketing and manufacturing centre for Eastern
Africa. International capital thus changed the character of the
economy of the colony, which was no longer totally dependent on
agriculture. In the new circumstances, existing economic structures,
which gave settlers monopoly control of marketing, prices and
in-puts, seemed out-dated and needlessly expensive and wasteful.
Racial barriers hindered capitalist accumulation in the colony and
limited African productivity. Britain could no longer afford to
prop up a small parasitic caste. 'White Man's Country' would have
to go the way of all uneconomic lost causes, and become the
subject of nostalgic reminiscences over drinks at the Club and in
books about 'Happy Valley'.

The post-war international situation thus demanded a new
approach to the exploitation of our people. Foreign capitalists
made it a policy to create an African middle-class which could
mediate their needs and consume their commodities. Since the
1920s a small group of Kenyans had been pushing to become
exactly that. Men whose education had enabled them to become
teachers and clerks had hoped to put their salaries, however small,
to commercial use. But they were frustrated, mainly by licensing
regulations and colonial policy which barred them from obtaining
bank loans or any credit beyond 200 shillings. At the same time
they were prevented from growing cash-crops. The frustrations felt
by these more prosperous of our countrymen were reaching
dangerous proportions by the 1940s; it was time for the colonialists
to invite them in from the cold. The new governor from 1944 to
1952, Sir Philip Mitchell, made it his primary task to create
conditions for the consolidation of an African *petit-bourgeoisie*
which would work with, not against, the government.

The Mitchell Approach

Mitchell's plan for 'multi-racialism' in Kenya obviously had
nothing to do with African self-rule. Mitchell himself was a firm
believer in the doctrine of trusteeship, maintaining that Africans
would not be ready for independence for 2,000 years, possibly a
little less. But he knew the settler approach, which doomed the
African population to an eternity of service, was potentially
ruinous, both economically and politically. He favoured a so-called
pluralistic approach to economic development, in which African
economic interests would, for the first time, be taken into account.
Recognizing the potential of peasant production, he pushed for
the creation of a prosperous peasantry and a halt to the alarming
deterioration of land in the 'reserves'. As for the wage sector, he
urged that Africans be turned into a genuine urban proletariat,
earning a 'proper' wage which would enable them to lessen their
dependence on the 'reserves' for subsistence. Mitchell believed a
prosperous and stable Kenya depended on the advancement of
the capitalist mode of production and class formation. Under his
scheme, land would be consolidated, with rich Africans buying
out their poorer brothers. The rich would then go into trade,
after racial barriers regulating commerce were removed. They
would collaborate with the colonialists, and mediate the intensification of African cash-crop production. The poor would leave the
'reserves' for the towns, where they would settle into a full-time
urban existence, providing a labour force for the new
manufacturing enterprises -- the *giriminti*, *kibarua*, and *jaguti*.
Mitchell, and the Labour Party Colonial Secretary, Creech Jones,
hoped that intensified capitalist forces and relations of
production in the colonies would give the impoverished Mother
Country a much-needed economic boost.

However, neither Mitchell nor Creech Jones nor their successors
cared to face the political implications of their new economic
policies. They could not, as they intended, sanction the creation
of an African *petit-bourgeoisie* and then deny it a meaningful
political voice. But this was what they tried to do. To the Governor,
even moderate Kenyans appeared dangerous radicals with
'Communist' connections. The British administration greatly
feared the awakening of nationalism among their subject peoples
in Africa and Asia. They suspected that 'Communism' might be
imported into Kenya by the returning soldiers. Africans who were
not working for national independence but for personal opportuni-

ties within the colonial framework were not to be trusted. Thus, Mitchell turned a deaf ear to the moderates in the Kenya African Union (KAU), when they assured him that 'our peoples are not yet ripe to carry the responsibilities of a self-governing country.'

So spoke KAU in 1946. Not all Kenyans were so deferential or submissive to British authority. Then, as now, we had among us the time-servers and the opportunists, but we also had among us brothers and sisters in their thousands who were prepared to die for the liberation of our country. These men and women, soon to take to the forest as the Kenya Land Freedom Army, wrote a new chapter in our long tradition of resistance to colonial domination.

The Birth of Our Power

The earliest days of imperialist take-over witnessed fierce uprisings among the Giriama, the Kikuyu, the Nandi, the Kamba, the Gusii, the Turkana. When the uprisings were brutally suppressed by the superior fire-power of the invaders, our peoples found other ways to protest their loss of freedom. Protest movements taking a religious guise were common in Ukambani and western Kenya. Overtly political demonstrations dated from the formation of the nation-wide East African Association, and the Thuku 'riot' of 1922. From 1922 to 1952 our peoples used all the peaceful means at their disposal to resist their subjugation. Many refused to submit tamely to ideological control and western values, but instead formed associations, started newspapers, and their own schools and break-away religious groups to assert African cultural integrity.

Protests were not merely regional, nor purely racial. Despite British attempts to encourage purely 'tribal' divisions in order to fragment the people, during the 1930s and 1940s there was a ground-swell of anti-colonialist sentiment which transcended ethnic divisions and enabled Africans and Asians from various parts of Kenya to organize themselves to fight together for their common interests as workers and victims of colonial oppression. Asians like Isher Dass, M.A. Desai, and later Makhan Singh and Pio Pinto, were especially prominent in publicizing grievances through newspapers, and the trade union movement which grew vigorously in the 1930s. The unions, using with considerable effectiveness the weapon of the general strike, organized labour on a *class* — not ethnic, racial or occupational — basis. Their leaders fought to retain their independence of action, and refused to be co-opted by the colonial administration.

By the late 1930s and 1940s there were organizational links between the unions in the towns and the majority of our people in the countryside. Resistance to various aspects of colonial policy was often nation-wide. For instance, the trade unions, and such organizations as the Kenya African Union (K.C.A.), the Kavirondo Taxpayers Welfare Association, the Ukamba Members Association, the Taita Hills Association, and the North Kavirondo Central Association, all took up the issue of land alienation and demanded a better deal for the African people. Protests became more militant after World War II. Nationalist feeling nurtured by such bodies as the Forty Group, the Action Group within KAU, and the unions under Chege Kibachia and Makhan Singh, must be seen as part of a general world-wide Afro-Asian movement against colonial domination. As the militants mobilized people in the towns, and among the squatters in the Rift Valley to struggle for their liberation, the moderates gave more hesitant support to the nationalist movement. They wanted the way cleared for their further self-enrichment, and saw such an opportunity under African majority-rule.

By 1950, militants and moderates in the nationalist movement were, as we shall see later, uneasy allies. The moderates preferred to negotiate, the militants — aware of the devious nature of the colonialists — wanted to *fight* for their independence. By 1952, the militants were in open insurrection, and the administration, with the implicit support of moderates like Eliud Mathu, had retaliated with the declaration of a State of Emergency which was to last until January 1960.

This is not the place to list the unspeakable brutalities inflicted upon the Kenyan people during these years. Suffice it to say that the war of liberation fought by our people has not yet been fully or properly documented from the Kenyans' point of view. Most Kenyan historians are notoriously timid when it comes to the subject of the Emergency and Mau Mau. For reasons of intrigue and personal pettiness most of them dismiss the achievements of the Kenya Land Freedom Army in Corfield style, refusing to admit that it had nation-wide support and aimed at nation-wide independence. To see our liberation struggle as the manifestation of purely Kikuyu frustrations is to play into the hands of the colonial rulers and their African successors with a stake in dividing the country on 'tribal' lines. Non-Kenyan historians have, for the

most part, relied in their histories of Mau Mau on official information and British-supplied data. The official figure of 11,000 dead
should, on a conservative estimate, be tripled at least. The
chronicle of atrocity and bestiality perpetrated by British soldiers
and their Kenyan lackeys lives on in the minds of our parents.
Some day soon their testimony must become part of our national
heritage. Too long has it been slighted by a ruling clique anxious
to disguise the heinous origins of its prosperity and political power.

Those who emerged to rule us in 1963 were, in many cases, those
who had betrayed our freedom fighters. They were the loyalists,
whose co-operation with the murderers of our people bought them
privileges and wealth. Loyalists were exempt from certain fees
and taxes. They could move around freely, without a pass, while
their suffering kinsmen were imprisoned in camps and 'protected
villages'. They had access to land consolidation committees where
they could put forward their own personal interests. They alone,
among the African population of Central Province, could plant
cash-crops and own trading plots. Under the point system they
got more votes per individual in the 1957 elections, which produced
a Bishop Muzorewa-style future ruling elite.

The loyalists were the chief beneficiaries of the Swynnerton
Plan, which put into action Mitchell's scheme for expanded
capitalist production in the colony. The Swynnerton Plan aimed
at the consolidation and registration of land in the 'reserves' on a
freehold tenure basis, in order to enable the 'reserves' to absorb
thousands of Kenyans repatriated from Tanganyika and other parts
of the colony, where it was feared they would spread Mau Mau
feeling. During consolidation in Central Province, begun in 1955,
half the land was awarded to less than 2% of the population.
Those in a position to buy land from the poor became even richer
once the restrictions of African coffee-growing were removed.
The poor became landless.

By the end of the Emergency the colonial government had
succeeded in creating a puffed-up African middle class, a group of
nascent grabbers and looters whose prosperity grew out of
treachery to our people. Such people shared the aspirations of
the British. Their goal was to possess businesses or settler-style
mixed farms, frequented by settler golf and business partners.
They shared with the foreigners an interest in stamping out the
revolutionary energy of our people. They could be trusted to make
'independence' safe for the continued operations of international
capital.

Towards 'Independence'

By 1960, some form of independence had become inevitable. International capital had deserted the settlers, who had simply become too expensive to support. America, looking to expand her trade and investments with Africa and Asia, pressured Britain to disentangle herself from the Empire. Granting 'independence' made good political and economic sense to the imperialists, once they had created a tame collaborating class with an interest in 'smooth transition'.

After 1963, the losers were those who had fought for liberation, the winners those eager to 'eat'. The African President assured the former colonial rulers that 'the government of an independent Kenya will not be a gangster government'. A 'gangster government' was presumably one which would repossess the stolen lands for the use of all the people and preside over the creation of a more egalitarian society. Kenyatta's government instead turned its back on the question of land transfer without compensation. Africans were made to purchase land at inflated prices, with money lent by the British government and the World Bank. Loan repayments then forced them into perennial indebtedness and poverty. Many of our people could not afford to buy land. Excluded from land consolidation schemes because of their sympathy with the freedom struggle, they were to remain landless in Kenyatta's Kenya.

Thus, at independence the stress was on continuity, as the new politicians, civil servants, large farmers, traders, industrialists and other businessmen, closed their ranks against the mass of our people and their demands for land and justice. The structure of the colonial economy and political system — as we shall see in the next chapter — was transferred virtually intact to Kenyans who preached harmonious co-existence with the exploiters of Kenya. Our bogus independence must be seen as a victory for the imperialists, and a demonstration of the ease with which international capital could bend nationalism to its own ends.

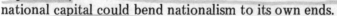

2. KANU and Kenyatta: Independence for Sale

Put this at end.

Definitely pivot to this, word count careful.

Kenya has never achieved true independence. Full independence can only be brought about by revolution. It is the culmination of popular, protracted revolutionary change, during which the people seize control of the instruments of power under the leadership of a party dedicated to the eradication of the institutions and forms of the colonial state. In Amilcar Cabral's words, 'it is necessary to totally destroy, to break, to reduce to ash all aspects of the colonial state' before independence can be achieved. Colonial domination must be demolished through active popular struggle. No colonial ruling power has ever voluntarily relinquished hegemony at a negotiating table. It will only consent to negotiate if it can, in the long term, either preserve or even extend its position of privilege through bargaining. Such was the intention of the British when they prepared to hand over nominal power to Kenyans at the Lancaster House Conference. The terms on which they handed over 'power' demonstrated, that in one guise or other, they intended to stay in Kenya.

Independence means self-determination and self-government. An independent nation is one with the autonomy to make decisions which will advance the welfare of its people. It is a nation that controls its own resources, and has the political and economic scope to utilize these resources, human and natural, free of foreign interference.

Independence in this sense has little relevance to our current situation. We find ourselves enclosed in a dependent country, wholly subservient to foreign interests. Our economy is geared to the needs of foreigners — both of our ex-colonial masters and other Western capitalist nations. In order to keep things that way our people are deprived of vital human freedoms, including the right of political self-expression and association. 'Neo-colonialism' is not

Put at end.

merely a matter of academic debate (and in any case there is very little of that) in Kenya. It is a condition which our people live with day by day: a form of oppression every bit as effective as that practised by British colonialists. In the last 20 years, our aspirations for political redress and economic reconstruction have been strangled. The sense of power we possessed when we took up arms against colonialism in the 1950s has been undermined and stifled. We are told that 'politics' came to an end in 1963. Now that we have our *uhuru* we must 'forget the past'. We have no need to discuss issues — discussion is dangerous 'rumour-mongering'. All we need is unquestioned loyalty to our gang of leaders, and a mute faith in their ritual incantation of 'peace, love and unity'.

Big Boss Politics

As the gulf between minority rich and the mass of poor continues to widen, we are told that there are no divisions in our country which cannot be healed by 'peace, love and unity', and a tame obedience and silence on our part. What passes for 'political' life revolves entirely around personalities who serve as our bosses, our patrons. They are far from representing our true interests. Instead, they represent, at the local level, the power of the *big boss*, the all-powerful sun of the system around which the politicians rotate like planets. All power radiates from the centre of the system, from our imperial President. Political success and personal enrichment depend on the positions held by the different planets as they circulate around the sun-king. Since the President, through his control of the state apparatus, bestows access to our country's increasingly scarce resources, the closer the politician-planet to the centre, the more power he can trap and reflect on down to his own satellites and flunkeys. As our politicians orbit endlessly around the President, they compete with each other to sing his praises loudly and attract his favour. Obsequious loyalty brings its own reward — a position closer to the warming power of the sun with all the economic privileges that go with membership of the inner circles. A loss of favour could put the politician out of orbit altogether, into limbo or extinction.

Such is the nature of Kenyan 'politics' today. Like an earlier sun-king, this President professes to rule by divine right, as the chosen of God. He, too, has his court and jesters. He exercises supreme authority by mumbled decree, his every murmur being

sacrosanct until it is found to be unworkable, ruinous, or both.
Politicians and appointed officials carry out the imperial will.
Their chief function is to smother all debate, and to link the
people firmly into a boss-servant chain of relationships which
constitutes our permitted political life. The keys to the chain are
the D.O.s, D.C.s, and P.C.s: they operate a rigid licensing system
through which the government controls all gatherings of the people
— no licence, no meeting, no matter how innocent. Surveillance
practised by the Special Branch, C.I.D., and G.S.U. destroys not
only any vestige of 'participatory democracy', but also, as we shall
see later, our people's own initiative to better their condition. In
Kenya today any such initiative is always deemed subversive.

Of course, as in other repressive regimes there are, from time to
time, elections of a sort which allow 'friendly' foreign nations the
opportunity to hold Kenya up as the show-piece of 'democracy' in
Africa. These elections are totally devoid of debate on issues.
Instead, all campaigning centres upon weak, generally corrupt,
safe personalities who have the KANU seal of approval. The
winners are usually those most adept at the intimidation and/or
bribery of voters. Elections do, however, fulfil a useful function, as
far as the government is concerned; they provide it with fresh packs
of 'eaters' willing to carry out government policy, against the
interests of their constituents if necessary.

These victorious politicians are, in practice, accountable to the
President alone, who has various methods of keeping them in
line. Elected M.P.s who attempt to represent the wishes of their
constitutents against government policy find that Parliamentary
immunity is an empty concept in Kenya. Parliament itself is a
jokers' forum, which can be ignored, ridiculed, or dismissed out of
hand if 'unruly'.

As for our one official party, the party which supposedly won
us 'independence', it has long been in a stupor. No political
initiative or policy-making emanates from KANU, a 'party' without
regular party machinery or even functioning local branches. KANU
today fulfils two functions, neither reputable. Since only those
Kenyans wealthy enough to afford to buy life membership can be
elected party officials, it serves as a rich man's club, whose members
are dedicated to making themselves even richer. From time to
time, party branches are resuscitated in order to counter moves
made by political dissidents or those slow in expressing their
loyalty to the President and his clique. To further confound those
who believed that parties like KANU should represent and respond

15

to the needs of the people, KANU, in 1979, was declared to be 'above the law'. It thus became a tool of a President himself 'above the law' and beyond all criticism, even by elected representatives of the people. The President and his closest associates can — and do — indulge in any kind of skullduggery without fear of the courts. With party functions reduced to 'eating' and arm-twisting, with a legislature and judiciary whose autonomy and integrity have been subverted, with a President who rules as a kind of sultan, political life in Kenya today is a complete negation of what we fought to attain. The rulers of 'independent' Kenya could have taught their colonial predecessors a thing or two about how to keep down the natives.

Did we fight for *uhuru* in order to be politically silenced in a supposedly free Kenya? To be intimidated, detained, and even eliminated for reminding our so-called leaders that they are there to represent *our* interests and not merely their own? To be ruled by a virtual king and his gang of favourites, all above the law and beyond the reach of principle and social responsibility? At what point did the party in which we once vested our hopes for the future become little more than a source of jobs and loot for politicians and their hangers-on? KANU's failure to function as a forum for political expression is symbolized today by an empty office in the Kenyatta Conference Centre: was it a pseudo-party from the beginning?

Enter KANU

The idea of forming the Kenya African National Union (KANU) was born at the 1960 Lancaster House Conference in London on the prospects for majority rule in Kenya. In the turbulent 1950s, Kenyans had been allowed district, but not nation-wide political associations, with all political parties being banned between June 1953 and June 1955. In an effort to overcome the divide-and-rule tactics deployed by the British in their support for the Kenya African Democratic Union (KADU), the originators of KANU in May 1960 combined district associations into a national party. KANU promised to usher in full independence for the peoples of Kenya.

The party seemed to be off to a rousing start. It had leaders: Kenyatta, languishing in detention, was surrounded by an almost mythical aura. It had branches: the old district associations. More

crucially, it had the enthusiastic support of people who believed it
to be the vehicle for bringing home independence. And finally,
it had a stirring party programme. Delivered in the form of a
political 'manifesto' to a huge rally at Thika on 20 November
1960, the *KANU Manifesto for Independence, Social Democracy
and Stability* makes instructive, and ironic, reading today. Before
the jubilant crowd the party proclaimed that

> all privileges and vestiges of colonialism will be swept away.
> Freedom has no meaning without the provision of the means
> for the vast majority of the people to enjoy that freedom.

KANU promised to replace the colonial regime with 'a political
democracy' which would be concerned to safeguard the 'good of
the country as a whole and not merely the interests of a few'.
Such a 'political democracy' would, the party affirmed, always
seek to mobilize 'the greatest possible element of consent' and
support from below.

Which Kenyan can read the *Manifesto* today without a bitter
laugh? How mocking seem the firm pledges made by KANU 20
years ago; how swiftly were the pledges broken. For instance, in
1960 the party vowed always to be dynamic — a promise which it
kept perhaps until 1963, when it practically ceased to function as
anything other than a tool to be used to remove the politically
undesirable. It made a number of other pledges equally ironic in
retrospect. Thus, it promised to work for 'the good of the country
as a whole and not merely the interests of a few. It vowed to have
nothing to do with the 1959 Detention Act, and other 'undemo-
cratic, unjust and arbitrary practices'. It declared its intention to
do away with P.C.s, D.C.s, and chiefs, and replace their rule by
institutions through which the people could exercise the 'right of
self-government'. It pledged itself to end the racist practice whereby
Africans were stopped on the streets and asked to produce their
identity cards, and it attacked 'artificial restrictions on the movement of produce from district to district coupled with monopolistic
control exercised over them' which, in its view, caused 'sky-
rocketing prices of the commodities which are the staple food of
the African people'. It took a populist line on housing as well as
food distribution, maintaining that 'before citizen E has 20 rooms
to protect him from rain, citizen A must have shelter'. In short,
through its *Manifesto* KANU expressed its firm intention to develop
Kenya 'into a prosperous welfare state', an intention which, like

so many others, is further away from realization than ever. Today the document appears as a testament to what might have been: a *Manifesto* for a still-born party which for most of its official 'life' has been little more than a corpse.

The founders of KANU seem to have been blind to the fact that there is more to the formation of a party than the adoption of a name. A party is really only worthy of the name 'party' if it acts to animate and then channel popular expression at all levels of society. Despite its appearance of health and a certain measure of unanimity in 1960, KANU was never, in fact, a vertically-integrated party tapping and giving voice to grass-roots interests. Instead, in Odinga's words, it remained an 'amalgam of many diverse tendencies and policies', a mere 'union' of different and even antagonistic interests. In the *Manifesto* of 1960, KANU acknowledges that it is more of a coalition (by implication, temporary) than anything else — it presents itself as a 'united front' composed of Kenyans joined together by the one common goal of working for independence. As our country was shortly to discover, there could be many different things meant by 'independence'.

Militants and Moderates

At the risk of some over-simplification, we can say that the 'amalgam' which was KANU contained two broadly different groups. On one side were people who believed that 'independence' necessitated a total break with the colonial system and a new beginning. They realized that a new beginning was only possible if Kenyans themselves had control of the country's resources and political destiny. For our purposes here we can call this group of radicals the militant nationalists. Their voice set the tone of the 1960 KANU *Manifesto*, demanding a clean break with the past and the creation of a more egalitarian society in the future through such devices as free education for all and a ceiling on how much private property one individual can own. Despite the attempt made by the colonial government — and later by the 'independent' government — to label them as such, these nationalists were by no means socialists. Nowhere did they speak out against the institution of private property, but they did maintain that a certain amount of nationalization of the country's resources and the serious encouragement of co-operative farming would benefit the Kenyan people as a whole. Their message presented in the

18

Manifesto was that wealth and power in Kenya should *not* be monopolized by the few, as under the colonial regime. The new beginning demanded by independence should widen opportunities for all Kenyans, and give the people as a whole a meaningful political role.

But the other broad group within the 'amalgam' was ultimately to win the day. These were the moderate nationalists, who stressed *continuity* with the past, and not a complete break with the colonial system. They wanted to be well placed to take over positions vacated by the departing British, and to maintain the pattern and direction of colonial rule. Early in 1960 they were willing to allow the radicals to set the rhetorical tone of the *Manifesto* in order to win widespread popular support, making sure, however, that the 'Kenya for Kenyans' style of rhetoric was confined to what were essentially *secondary* issues. On the vitally important *primary* issues — of the land, and of foreign investment — they were determined to push through their own policies.

Land was the touchstone of new government policy. It was the means of production for the vast majority of our people, and the source of a bitter sense of grievance during the colonial period. With the nearing of 'independence', the people demanded the return of the stolen lands as a matter of justice. They saw no need to pay compensation to settlers who had come as thieves. In Kaggia's words 'it looks very absurd for Africans to buy land that was rightly theirs.' But the moderates felt otherwise, and significantly, wrote their view into the *Manifesto*. KANU as a party accepted 'the principle of fair and just compensation', despite the fact that such a principle ran directly counter to the needs and interests of the people. There would be no 'free things' in an African-run Kenya.

Nor would there be any radical departure in economic thinking. The moderates asserted in the *Manifesto* that 'development' would continue along *the same lines*, making the implicit assumption that colonial style 'development' was in fact the real thing. The *Manifesto* voiced the radical pledge to resettle landless Africans, but 'not at the cost of the high standard of agriculture already attained, and which must continue.' A KANU government would continue to approach economic matters in much the same old way, heavily emphasizing the dubious benefits of large mixed farming. Continuity was not to be confined to agriculture. The *Manifesto* also reassured agents of international capital that there would be no change at 'independence', but 'both public and private enterprise,

local or from overseas, have a sure place in Kenya's development.'
Investment from all sources would be encouraged and protected.

What conclusions can we draw from the evidence offered by
the 1960 KANU *Manifesto*? We can say that as early as 1960 the
militant nationalists were outflanked by the group which was
subsequently to inherit the trappings of political power — the
moderates. The militants had on their side a strong commitment
to the independence of our country, which won them the support
of most Kenyans. They had a populist rhetoric, and a sense of
indignation at the way Kenyans were exploited by foreign interests
which enabled them to sway crowds.

Furthermore, they had the support of a grass-roots organization,
the *Kiama kia Muingi* (KKM), which was a regrouping of former
members of the Kenya Land Freedom Army. The KKM was
committed to 'free land', through active seizures if necessary. It
planned to capture political control of KANU's rural branches, and
also to collect arms as insurance against a 'sell-out' at 'independence'.
The great weakness of the KKM was organizational. When Kenyatta
chose to move against its members in 1961, he easily isolated the
leaders, and detained key cadres. The decapitation of KKM left
the militant nationalists without an organizational base. They
remained a minority faction within KANU, having failed to create
their own sources of funds, their own propaganda organs, and
institutionalized popular support. Their programme won majority
favour, but they had no ability to carry it out. Kenya's radicals
on the verge of 'independence', therefore, suffered from the same
near-sightedness which has afflicted all opposition spokesmen
since. They displayed a lack of political judgment, and ignorance
of the nature of political struggle. They were easily isolated and
neutralized; and, as the mainstream of Kenya's political history
passed them by, made to seem irrelevant.

In 1960, the mainstream within KANU was flowing strongly
towards the shores of neo-colonialism. The moderates, therefore,
had their say on the primary economic issues which committed
Kenya to continuity, not to change. The colonial model, minus
such irritants as the legal colour bar, would be preserved in
'independent' Kenya.

Mitchell's Children

There is nothing surprising in this result of a *negotiated* handover
of power. For more than a decade — ever since the governorship
of Philip Mitchell — British and foreign interests had been working
to produce just such a result. As we saw in the last chapter,
Mitchell and his successors wanted to 'modernize' the colonial
economy in order to make it reflect new international realities.
Essentially, this meant doing away with the so-called 'dual economy',
in which African subsistence farming existed side by side with
European cash-crop production. As Mitchell realized, the integration
of African production into the 'modern' sector would enormously
advance the interests of capitalism and raise the productivity of
the colony as a whole. As we have seen, Mitchell thus opted for
the creation of an African middle class, and the raising of rural
productivity in order to overcome the stagnation endemic in an
economy geared simply to minority settler interests. The Swynnerton Plan and Dow Commission embraced these goals, seeking to
modernize agriculture through the consolidation of holdings and
granting of freehold titles.

Mitchell's new economic policy did not only concern itself with
peasant farming in rural areas. He also invited in foreign capital in
increasing quantities. As in West Africa, where giant firms like
Unilever had successfully pioneered the strategy of grooming
African managers and executives who could be reliable political
partners as well, Mitchell and his successors sought to implement
the policy of 'multi-racialism' in business and the civil service. From
the early 1950s a series of Commissions examined ways of freeing
the economy from racial restrictions, in the name of political
stability. Businessmen like Sir Philip Rogers, the first president of
the Association of Commercial and Industrial Employers (later the
Federation of Kenya Employers) and director of British American
Tobacco, drew on their varied West African experience when they
set about creating a group of reliable 'African allies' in Kenya.
Their type of 'multi-racialism' became the watchword of liberal
organizations like the United Kenya Club and the Capricorn Society,
and the hope for the future of Blundell's New Kenya Group.
'Multi-racialism' depended on the emergence of trustworthy
African successors to the colonial rulers who were well aware that
their time was running out. The future, in their eyes, was one in
which a white and black bourgeoisie with common interests would
work together to defeat militant nationalism, and ensure that

21

'independence' meant continuity, not change.

This strategy was to pay off handsomely. The KANU politicians who became our rulers in 1963 were the up-and-coming accumulators whose economic interests will be described in the next chapter. They had the weight of the 'progressive' foreign business community and 'liberal' colonial opinion behind them. Given the political weakness of their opponents, their emergence to power in 'independent' Kenya was practically assured. By the early 1960s, all sources of organized opposition to a neo-colonial solution had been isolated: they were shortly to be reduced to opposition in Parliament and rendered impotent. The KKM was suppressed. The unions, which in the early 1950s had played a significant political role in fighting colonialism, were made politically harmless, as workers were gradually deprived of a sense of their *class* interests. In the late 1940s and early 1950s unions had stood out against tribalism and racialism. During the Emergency, however, with the detention of far-sighted union leaders like Makhan Singh, and the mass round-up and detention of the urban Kikuyu population, the government used divide-and-rule tactics to break union solidarity. 'Tribalism' was used to divide the work-force, and keep workers from re-organizing on class lines.

At the same time, labour leaders like Tom Mboya argued that unions should *not* be a political force in Kenya, but should merely work for bread-and-butter issues. Mboya himself was a classic example of the 'new' upwardly mobile Kenyan, dedicated to making the most of opportunities offered by a multi-racial Kenya. As general secretary of the Kenya Federation of Labour from 1953, he brought the unions into line with Western (especially American) interests. The International Confederation of Free Trade Unions (ICFTU) had been formed in 1949 by Western industrialized nations under American leadership to counteract Soviet influence in the trade union movement. In 1951, the ICFTU moved into East Africa and played a major role, with Mboya's connivance, in educating Kenyan unionists to see things America's way. Mboya himself had a flair for tapping American funds for the Kenya Federation of Labour. As its general secretary, as well as KANU's general secretary, Mboya was in a powerful position during Kenya's transition to 'independence'. He subsequently became Kenya's Labour Minister and the originator of the anti-union Central Organisation of Trade Unions (COTU), which was a government-run workers' confederation dedicated to preventing strikes and keeping 'industrial peace'. As the organizer of the

American-sponsored 'air-lifts' of Kenyan students, Mboya also played an important role in helping foreign capital recruit and groom its future collaborators from among our youth.

Enter Kenyatta

'New' men like Mboya, eager to take advantage of the opportunities offered by the new economic and political order, needed an 'old' nationalist figurehead who would see things their way. Jomo Kenyatta, conveniently in detention in 1960, was a man of the appropriate stature. Insisting on this gave the nationalists, and KANU in particular, a useful uniting slogan. To the writers of the KANU *Manifesto* Kenyatta himself symbolized unity:

> Kenyatta's great popularity and moral authority among all people will enable us to overcome these strains and stresses and to secure the unity of the nation by smashing the tribalists.

The militant nationalists made a great mistake by rallying around the symbol of Kenyatta, believing that they could harness his prestige to their own purposes. They should have known better, for Kenyatta had long shown himself to be the foe of both militant nationalism and the voice of the people. By nature a dictator, in the colonial period he specialized in killing popular debate and advancing his own cause instead of his countrymen's. He had proved himself through the years to be a thorough opportunist more than willing to live off the people's support and adulation. Determined to be *THE* boss, Kenyatta could not tolerate political rivalry or even discussion. Nor could he countenance the activity of popular organizations over which he had no control. Thus, in 1946 he denounced Chege Kibachia for leading a general strike of trade union members in Mombasa, believing that unions should be apolitical and moderate in their economic demands. Subsequently, he tried to thwart the wishes of Kenyans determined to use all means at their disposal to fight for independence, and found himself on the Mau Mau death list for his dangerous compromising. His detention was in fact a form of protective custody.

Kenyatta in detention was a useful national symbol for KANU, and a hope to the radicals that they would eventually win the day.

From Kenyatta's own point of view, spending the early transition period in detention might have been irksome and uncomfortable, but it had some rewards. Marooned in Lodwar and then Maralal, Kenyatta was initially saved from having to take a political stand on the most critical issues of the day — the question of land for the landless and the fate of the 'White Highlands'.

While Kenyatta was waiting offstage, KANU's leaders and the colonial government were hammering out a solution to the land problem, which betrayed the mass of our people and set the stage for continued co-operation between a parasitic ruling class and the international bourgeoisie. In 1960 and 1961, there was growing pressure on the colonialists and nationalists alike to do something about the landless. 1961 was a year of famine, with conditions in the 'reserves' made worse by the return of those men and women who had spent the Emergency in detention. Not surprisingly, a radical grass-roots alternative to KANU seemed to be making rapid headway, as squatters and landless joined the KKM in large numbers. In some cases, they refused to await the compromise solution being reached by KANU and the British on land, and instead, seized the land from settlers for their own use. In order to forestall rapidly growing discontent some type of resettlement scheme was clearly a political necessity.

Buying Back Our Land

This is the background to the call made by militant nationalists like Kaggia and the organizers of the KKM: Kenyans should not, they insisted, be forced to buy land that was rightfully theirs. In May 1961, on the outskirts of Nairobi, Odinga addressed a crowd of nearly 20,000 which collectively vowed never to *buy* land in the Highlands. But growing militancy on this all-important issue was successfully undermined by KANU moderates and British de-colonizers. The pro-British land formula which they agreed upon represented the most critical compromise of the 'independence' negotiations. They would attempt to buy political stability through a token resettlement programme, while at the same time forcing Africans to buy the land and disguising the impact of this policy with 'release Kenyatta' diversions.

Kenyatta, finally released from custody in mid-1961, had, by early 1962, thrown his weight solidly behind the moderates in KANU: 'we do not believe in being given this or that free,' he told a Legislative Council meeting in January 1962 in his capacity as President of KANU. He added that land should be purchased by Africans, so that property rights would be respected. Shortly afterwards, the Million Acre Settlement Scheme was announced by the colonial government (July 1962). Under this scheme, part of the Highlands would be sub-divided and sold to 30,000 landless families. The country had to repay the British and World Bank loans which over-compensated departing settlers. Thanks to KANU's blundering, we began our 'independence' already in debt and faced a future rigged against our fundamental national interests.

In immediate terms, however, those landless families which got access to land through the scheme thought themselves fortunate. The Settlement Scheme was essentially a way of de-politicizing a potentially explosive situation. Some land in the Highlands was sold to the landless in order to buy security for the large number of Highland farms, which either remained in settler hands or passed to the African comprador bourgeoisie. The Million Acre Scheme was, therefore, a way of pre-empting political strife, and one in accord with the moderate nationalist stress on continuity, not change. The existing colonial agricultural framework of large mixed farms and numerous small-holdings was transferred more or less intact to 'independent' Kenya. There was of course a cosmetic difference — the former 'White' Highlands were now the 'multi-racial' Highlands. Newly in possession of vast tracts of land, African mixed farmers came to share the settler economic outlook and aspirations. They, too, were in full agreement that 'growth' and 'development' should take precedence over welfare programmes. As for the new small-holders, they were to find themselves trapped in a cycle of poverty and debt. Settlement schemes were always economically marginal, since few small-holders could afford in-puts like fertilizer. But as far as the authorities were concerned, the formula of settling the landless while making them pay for it was a political triumph. The land issue could no longer be used in quite the same way by radical politicians, since it could now be shown that *something* was being done to help the landless. With the tacit support of African moderate nationalists, the transition government had no qualms about moving against the KKM and all people who refused to accept the compromising land policy. Ex-detainees were in many cases re-detained — squatters who boldly claimed land for themselves were imprisoned. Militant nationalists thus found themselves increasingly deprived of grass-roots support, and had no effective way to champion the people's interests. They had earlier put their hopes in Kenyatta's release, not realizing that he would become the main opponent of 'free things'.

Mtukufu Mzee

It seems that colonialists who had believed Kenyatta to be the 'manager of Mau Mau' had badly misread the man and his inclinations. After his release from detention in 1961 he soon convinced them of his firm friendship, becoming the 'leader unto darkness' and often 'death' only for the masses of Kenyans. As President, he soothed the settlers with the assurance that they had an important role to play in post-colonial Kenya. Such Presidential pronouncements as 'forgive and forget', 'suffer without bitterness', 'we all fought for independence, there is no Mau Mau and no Home Guards', 'mine is not a gangster government', and 'we need settler farmers to help us' were music to the ears of imperialists. In all his economic policy statements of 1963 Kenyatta went out of his way to show his disdain for militant nationalism and the wishes of the majority of Kenyans. He was determined to make foreign interests feel at home in 'independent' Kenya, and use them to enrich himself and his trusted political allies. The *Manifesto*'s 'one leader of great moral stature and enjoying universal respect' was soon to become the chief buccaneer of 'independent' Kenya, a thief whose appetite for loot earned him some international renown. But as long as he did not plunder *them*, international capitalists were pleased to accept his welcoming invitation. Kenyatta obliged them by frequently emphasizing his aversion to nationalization, and his respect for private property, free enterprise, and foreign investment.

Western capitals soon realized that Kenyatta was a true find: an African President who would be most unlikely to flirt with 'Communism'. As he created conditions for capitalist countries to have a free-for-all in Kenya, Kenyatta soon became a valuable ally in the fight against 'foreign ideology'. *Anything* which threatened imperialist control of our economy came into the category of 'foreign ideology'. Between Madaraka Day 1963 and the issuing of Sessional Paper No. 10 (on African Socialism) in 1965, the Americans and British tutored Kenyatta and the young KANU government on 'anti-Communist' tactics. 'Anti-Communism' was found to be thoroughly compatible with the official Kenyan ideology of 'African Socialism'. Sessional Paper No. 10 was based

on the Commonwealth Development Corporation's Gaitskill
Report, and the World Bank's *Economic Development of Kenya*.
Full of dubious concepts and ambiguities, the Paper enshrines the
views of international capitalism. Given the topsyturvey outlook
which to this day passes as official ideology, it is not surprising
to find the current Vice-President calling the sale to the public of
shares in companies a good 'socialist' measure, and the present
Minister for Constitutional and Home Affairs telling the Fourth
Parliament that an 'African Socialist' is an individualist, a
capitalist who wears a pin-striped suit.

Having found in Kenyatta a resolute champion of capitalism
and Western interests, neo-colonialist powers abandoned the
divide-and-rule tactics which had served as the rationale behind
majimbo and their initial support for KADU. They discovered
that a strongly centralized African government could serve their
interests more effectively. They soon got the strong government
they had been advocating through a rapid series of far-reaching
constitutional changes carried out between 1963 and 1968, which
wholly concentrated power in the person of the President, at the
expense of an independent judiciary, legislature, and people.
Many of the amendments pushed through during this five year
period were designed to oppose what was called a 'Communist'
threat to national security — more accurately, the attempt by
militant nationalists to use Parliament as a forum and instrument
to work for the true independence of the country.

Kenyatta, with the backing of the West, was the creator of the
imperial presidency. By December 1964, Kenya was a Republic,
with an executive who was both the head of State (replacing the
Queen) and the head of government. Subsequent constitutional
amendments relieved Parliament of any involvement in the election
and rulings of the President, and of any say over his conduct and
use of his power. The President was literally above the workings
of the law. Kenya was swiftly being transformed from the
'participatory Parliament' promised by the KANU *Manifesto* to a
personal dictatorship. Many of these amendments were of dubious
legality, even by the system's own equally dubious rules. The
Constitution became so 'amended' that by 1968 the old one was
discarded, and a new one written. The new Constitution, like the
old, was continually by-passed in the name of public security.
Parliament and the judiciary were progressively stripped of their
powers. For all practical purposes, the President, by late 1968 and
ever since, has been a kind of 'divine right' monarch — ruling by

decree, and often invoking God as his guide and the source of his power.

The President needed a bureaucracy to carry out his 'Royal Will'. He came to rely more and more on the authoritarian Provincial Administration, which in size and function represented a wholesale revival of the machinery of the Emergency. Under the Emergency, the colonial administration had been strictly centralized, with power flowing from the top down, and P.C.s serving as regional governors to carry out the colonial Governor's demands. At the local level, the colonial-appointed chief had the final say. The chief was responsible not to the people, but to the administration. It was exactly this method of 'ruling without politics' which the KANU *Manifesto* had so bitterly attacked in 1960: 'Agents of indirect rule, the P.C., D.C. and chiefs must go!' The *Manifesto* had promised to tear down the old colonial structures and put in their place 'participatory democracy' which, in its view, 'must include the greatest possible element of consent'.

KANU in the Closet

Kenya today has the trappings of a bourgeois democratic state, but certainly not the substance. Even before the transition period to 'independence' was over, KANU had shown itself incapable of being used as the vehicle of popular political expression, and by 1962 had virtually ceased to operate as a political organization. As far as the moderate nationalists who assumed control in 'independent' Kenya were concerned, KANU's 'united front' had served its function — it had provided a facade behind which moderates could out-manoeuvre those militant nationalists who were seeking to fulfil KANU's election promises. KANU had never possessed a smoothly-working party machinery, but under the first 'independent' regime the little machinery it *did* possess was completely neglected. Thus, there was not a single meeting of either the party national executive or governing council in the critical years of 1964 and 1965. The meetings which were subsequently held were entirely negative in character, with party officials being summoned specifically to carry out hatchet jobs on opponents of government policy. Without the least trace of procedural regularity in its functions, KANU became nothing more than a tool used by the President and his court to silence opposition. (See Appendix 1.) New regulations were soon passed dictating that anyone who intended to contest a Parliamentary seat obtain 'party clearance' and expensive life party membership — a provision which ensured that only the wealthy would rule the country.

For the new 'ruling class', party and State were to become instruments for unchecked personal accumulation and the plundering of the nation's resources. The powerful group which had captured the State included the comprador bourgeoisie and educated opportunists of all sorts, who willingly carried out World Bank/IMF strategies to keep Kenya safe for foreign investment. Any criticism of the governing gangsters and their sell-out policies was denounced as the work of 'Communists' who were envious of Kenya's 'progress' and 'stability', and bent on subversion.

Open Season on Militants

By the 1970s, few voices were raised against the ruling clique. Militant nationalism, confined largely to the back-benches of Parliament in newly 'independent' Kenya, did not survive the decade in any organized sense. By 1965, back-bench critics of the government had been labelled Communist subversives. Their most forceful leader, Pio Pinto, was murdered in February 1965. The government then cranked disused KANU machinery into life, and turned it against the remaining militant nationalists, who were ousted from the party at the Limuru Conference of 1966. Belatedly, they attempted to regroup, but their new opposition party, the KPU, was no match for a President now equipped with additional Emergency powers, and a ruthless willingness to use them.

KPU represented a somewhat forlorn, rearguard attempt by militant nationalists to revive the struggle for our elusive independence. Its denunciation of the rapacious ruling clique transcended 'tribal' lines. It sought, in a populist way, to articulate for *all* Kenyans an alternative to the massive betrayal of our people's true interests which constituted *Uhuru* under KANU and Kenyatta. But the individuals who attempted to rally the people against the Kenyatta regime were organizationally weak. Called 'snakes in the grass' by Kenyatta, KPU leaders were denied permits for their meetings — their supporters were harassed by the Special Branch and the G.S.U. A government-instigated mass shooting in Kisumu in 1969 gave Kenyatta the opportunity he needed to denounce the KPU as a purely Luo 'Communist-inspired' conspiracy against Kenya's so-called democratic government. Its leaders were detained, and the party itself banned. Certain constitutional amendments were then passed, at the bidding of the 'loyal' Luo, Tom Mboya, making Kenya a virtual one-party State, and prohibiting candidates from standing for any election without KANU's clearance.

During the decade following the banning of the KPU, the government moved steadily down the path to nascent fascism, using terror tactics to isolate and then eliminate dissidents. As Kenyatta dispensed with Cabinet meetings and other appearances of 'democracy', the government became the clique closest to the President — the Family and their hangers-on. Those who fattened themselves at Kenyatta's table had certain things in common. They were for the most part recruits from the Kikuyu bourgeoisie, whose historical origins we will consider in the next chapter. They had personal interests in the continued foreign domination of our country, and they were determined to safeguard those interests by winning the battle for Presidential succession.

To the regret of American imperialists, an early casualty in that battle was Mboya himself. Mboya had long been a faithful servant of the Kenyatta regime but as an outsider — and a popular one at that — he threatened the monopoly of power aimed at by the Family and its cronies, and thus had to be eliminated. In his various guises as trade union leader, Minister of Labour and then Minister of Economic Planning and Development, Mboya had been a precocious pupil in the Mitchell-Baring school for training 'new Kenyans'. Having mastered the lesson that Kenya's future development lay in neo-colonial economic and social arrangements, Mboya helped foreign interests consolidate their hold over the Kenyan economy. The United States especially found him a useful ally. A crusader against 'Communism' — whether embodied in literature, which now and then found its way into our country to 'pollute the virgin minds of our youth', or in the embattled ranks of the KPU — Mboya was America's rising star. His death, in 1969, at the hands of a government-paid assassin left Western policy-makers brooding about Kenya's future stability and searching for Mboya's replacement.

The West Closes In

That stability had assumed a growing importance in the calculations of the West. With Communism apparently on the march in
Asia, the capitalist camp was determined to make the Indian Ocean
region a bulwark against further Communist advance. For America
fighting a losing war in Vietnam, the implications of the 'domino
theory' had reached nightmare proportions. American strategists
used the coup in Zanzibar as an example of creeping Communism,
and an excuse to shore up its dominoes in Eastern Africa before
they all collapsed. Kenya, which had shown itself to be so
amenable to foreign control, was a key domino in the American
scheme of things. During the 1960s and 1970s it was important
because of its 'open door' policy toward international capital.
But it was even more important because of its adjacent position
to the warring countries in the Horn of Africa, a region whose
proximity to U.S. oil supplies in the Middle East brought it to the
attention of American policy-makers and arms dealers.

From the early 1960s, the American Ambassador William
Attwood had recognized the importance of wooing Kenyatta and
dictating his foreign policy. Mboya had been seen as an important
link-man in the extension of American influence over East Africa.
But by the end of the 1960s Mboya was dead, and Kenyatta was
old. As Kenyatta became senile and lost his grip on the running
of the country, would there be a possible resurgence of militant
nationalism seeking to reduce Western domination? Would
imperialist interests be sacrificed at the succession?

Capitalist countries, led by the United States, were determined
to prop up this particular domino. Throughout the 1970s, American
strategy in Kenya was aimed at bolstering the Old Man in his
dotage, and paving the way for a successor who would continue
the Kenyatta line. To this end, the C.I.A. gave Kenyatta a publicly-
reported $7 million to build an organization which could be used,
more effectively than the moribund KANU, to broaden and secure
his rule. Kenyatta chose to create a power base disguised as a
'welfare organization'. GEMA, supposedly just another welfare
union on the lines of the older Luo Union and New Akamba
Union, was actually a political and economic stronghold of the
Family and allies among the Kikuyu (especially the Kiambu
Kikuyu) bourgeoisie. GEMA, which from its initial formation was
rejected as *their* organization by the broad masses of the Kikuyu
people, served not only as the base for a new order of plundering

31

politicians and executives with international connections, but it
also, by the mid 1970s, acted informally as the Parliament, cabinet
and often the judiciary in the country. As we shall see later, its
leaders were able to use the apparatus of state — and Kenyatta's
name — to milk the people and emerge as the nation's foremost
power-brokers. Their link with Kenyatta assured them of limitless
opportunities for accumulation.

While imperialists had hoped that organizations such as GEMA
could be used to keep Kenya politically stable, the country was
in fact becoming increasingly factionalized. It would be a misreading
of the situation to see the deep divisions among our people as a
'natural' outcome of endemic 'tribalism'. Instead, our power-hungry
leaders stirred up and used tribal sentiment when they found it
convenient to do so. Thus, in the wake of Luo anger at Mboya's
murder, members of the ruling clique exploited the situation by
forced mass-oathing of the Kikuyu population at Gatundu, and the
appropriation of millions of shillings in oathing fees, causing
further dislike of GEMA in Kikuyuland as well as elsewhere.

The situation in 1969 and after should not be interpreted as a
straightforward Kikuyu vs Luo split. 'Tribalism' had instead been
cleverly used to divert attention from the real dynamics at work in
the country — the emergence of a rapacious bunch of mercenaries
whose own *class* interest transcended ethnic bounds. To their
credit, many of our people saw how they were being manipulated.
Thousands of Kikuyu, like the non-Kikuyu elsewhere, felt mounting
anger at the Gatundu oathing, at the role which nepotism played in
appointments, and at the way the Family and their associates seemed
to be grabbing all positions, property and power for themselves.
Factional rivalry — revolving around the divisions between 'eaters'
and 'non-eaters', or more often between 'big eaters' and 'small
eaters' — intensified during the 1970s, with general growing resentment at the strong-arm tactics of the Kiambu-based gang which was
determined to increase their influence with the President, and even
rule for him. Our public life degenerated into a series of ignoble
feuds among politicians eager to demonstrate their closeness to
Kenyatta in order to get their share of the pickings. The sheer
greed of the cabal closest to Kenyatta was outstripped only by
their unpopularity. As their appetites and bellies expanded, so did
their arrogance, until members of the inner circle felt they could
get away with literally anything. Their main concern was to keep
things that way. They were determined not to let the impending
death of the Old Man work against their interests.

Who's Next?

From the early 1970s, then, Kenyatta's senility was a prime factor in all political calculations. To the ruling clique, the 'national interest' had little to do with periodic famine, relentless inflation and the progressive impoverishment of the Kenyan people: it had everything to do with the succession. By the mid-1970s, our increasingly desperate people lost all hope that the existing system could be made responsive to their needs. That hope had been briefly rekindled when a group of back-benchers, including the popular J.M. Kariuki and J. Seroney, tried yet again to use Parliament as a forum to voice their criticisms of the regime. But the Third Parliament met for only one day in November 1974. Being immediately prorogued by Kenyatta, it did not meet again until February 1975. By the end of the month, J.M. Kariuki's attacks on the government and GEMA provoked them to retaliate in their traditional racketeer-style. JM's murder, a decade after the 'mysterious' killing of Pio Pinto, was meant to serve as a stern warning to remaining critics (and by then they were painfully few) of what to expect if they continued to find fault with the extravagant looting which had become a way of life to the men at the top.

The assassination of JM, and the government's clumsy attempt at a cover-up, unleashed the biggest political crisis which the regime had ever faced. Kenyatta went into hiding for two weeks, while riots occurred spontaneously in many towns. In Nairobi, demonstrating University students got vivid first-hand experience of the nature of a police State. Meanwhile, as part of the stifling of all protest, Parliament was thoroughly cowed. The report of the Parliamentary Committee set up to investigate JM's death was immediately suppressed, which was not surprising since it attributed the murder to the Family. In the aftermath of the suppression of the report, three M.P.s were detained and three others hauled up on staged 'criminal' charges. They ended up in jail, where they could meditate on the virtues of silence and loyalty. *Hansard*, the report of proceedings in Parliament, was tampered with to reflect the Family's view of things. Outside Nairobi, the Provincial Administration, Special Branch and G.S.U. went into action to detect and then crush opposition to the murderous regime. Such was the practice of 'parliamentary democracy' in Kenya in 1975.

From JM's death to Kenyatta's three and a half years later, all 'political' activity in the country revolved around silencing

dissidents and manoeuvring for the best standpoint from which to
wave the Old Man good-bye. Factional rivalry was intense between
members of the Family clique, and opponents clustered around the
Vice-President and Attorney-General. In no way can this rivalry be
interpreted as one between collaborators and true nationalists.
On the contrary, both sides had a considerable stake in maintaining
the general *status quo*. All contenders for power in the post-
Kenyatta era were members of the same broad self-interested overfed elite. What they were after was *not* a change in policy, but a
change in their own relative positions vis-a-vis the centre. Each
group wanted to control the Presidency, to be in the best position
to carry on where Kenyatta left off, and appropriate for themselves
and their political allies any remaining *matunda ya uhuru*.

Under the circumstances, KANU would have retained marginally
more dignity if it had remained comatose. But it was resurrected
to play an ignominious role in the struggle for succession, being
used as a debased tool by the clique around Kenyatta to eliminate
rivals. There were no elections for party posts for more than a
decade, because the Family and their allies in unpopularity could
not be certain that things would go their way. There were no
regular meetings of KANU, except illicit ones summoned to
further the schemes of the Family. The considerable resources
of GEMA were harnessed to the same end, as the Kiambu-based
gangsters and their flunkeys plotted to ensure that the Presidency
would not slip from their grasp.

But it did. Because of the manner and timing of Kenyatta's
death in August 1978, and because of the great unpopularity of
the Kenyatta clique, his Vice-President Moi, with the help of the
self-styled defender of the Constitution Charles Njonjo and the
former GEMA stalwart Mwai Kibaki, scraped through to the
Presidency. Surviving to become President has, it seems from the
present vantage point, taken all the cunning and political
shrewdness which Moi had at his command. These qualities have
rarely shown themselves since. Kenyatta, for all his greed and
crimes, *did* project certain attributes which made him a revered
figure among certain sections of the people. He appeared dignified,
competent, and charismatic, and retained the aura of the legendary
Grand Old Man of African nationalism. His successor clearly
lacks all of these qualities. In their place, we find indecisiveness
and bumbling on a spectacular scale. While Moi's manner of rule
by decree writes a new chapter in the history of incompetent
leadership, Kenyans are exhorted to follow in the wise ruler's

footsteps and learn the wisdom of total passivity. The puerile 'philosophy' of *nyayoism* is an insult to our people and an attempt to complete their political emasculation.

As the new king and his favourites amble around the countryside demanding adulation, gratitude and obeisance, they leave in their wake a national crisis of confidence which might prove their undoing. Some of the sheep have refused to follow! Some of the children have 'defied' the all-knowing father! For years the KANU government has simply ignored, repressed or lied about the major economic and social problems which we face. Like its predecessor, the *nyayo* government has operated on the principle that ruling is simply a matter of 'eating' and lapping up the praise, not of solving national problems. The President and his intimate cronies actually seem to *believe* the chorus of yes-saying which they have themselves orchestrated. KANU loudly proclaims that the President is above the law and above all criticism. Those who defy are traitors and criminals. The only language which the rulers bother to use is the language of the *rungu*.

As an illustration of the way the government creates national crises, take the case of the doctors. Unable to negotiate with a raised club, the government doctors, suffering a decade's unattended grievances, staged a spontaneous walk-out which the authorities countered by arresting them and their wives. Not content to harass them, and not about to sit down and discuss issues with them, the government then escalated the crisis by ordering that medical students be sent home. When other University students expressed their solidarity with the medical students and doctors, and sought redress of other longstanding problems, they were set upon by the G.S.U. and sent home 'indefinitely'. In the early stages of this government-made crisis, the authorities seemed to display the symptoms of advanced delusive paranoia. Totally isolated from reality, with no attempt to understand or come to terms with underlying problems, the government and its megaphone, KANU, have deliriously lashed out at 'Marxist lecturers', at 'foreign agitators', and at 'meddling politicians', blaming them for leading the flock astray. In a frenzy of rage at not being 'obeyed', the government has deprived various individuals of basic liberties and freedom of movement, and has arrested *Nation* newspaper journalists for writing reports implying that the government might not be in control of the situation. By so doing, they seem to be acting on the assumption that newspaper readers are mindless, and can be repeatedly duped and fooled into believing the government line. They thereby reveal their own stupidity. Do they really think, for instance, that students can be deterred from demonstrating in memory of JM by making certain that the University is closed on 2 March? Just as the authorities freely move Easter and Christmas around in order to shut the University when they wish, so the students will move JM day. (See Appendix 9). Meanwhile, as the national crisis enlarges, the government continues to throw tantrums and chant refrains about its infallibility. Regrettably, 20 years of KANU rule have created the conditions for a coup which, as things stand, can only hurry us down the road to national ruin.

3. Looters, Bankrupts and the Begging Bowl: Our Plundered Economy

All economic wealth is generated by three elements: 1) the personal activity of man or his *labour power*; 2) the *natural resources* of the earth (such as minerals, crops, energy), and 3) the *instruments* or machinery by which the labour power acts upon the resources to make products. The distinguishing feature of capitalism, as against all other systems of creating economic wealth, is that all these three elements — the means of production — are privately owned, generating a wealth which is privately owned. This wealth is distributed and disposed of by those who own these elements of production, not by the producers themselves. In Kenya, the labour power of the people and the natural resources of the land are largely owned and controlled by private interests, most of which are foreign-based.

The Kenyan economy is a deformed child of the international capitalist system. Since its 'coming of age' in 1963 it has given the outward appearance of growth, but inwardly has become more and more sickly. Its body, weakened and wasted by internal bleeding, is unable to regenerate organs which have atrophied. It has become increasingly feeble and incapable of feeding itself. Its dependence on the mother is now total. The question is how long will that mother — hardly one to be motivated by sentiment — take an interest in keeping alive so emaciated a specimen?

At present, the deformed and insignificant child is exposed without protection to the chill of the latest international capitalist crisis. It appears defenceless before predators which circle around to take whatever is going for their own survival. The seepage of blood from its body has become a haemorrhage. Its days seem numbered.

Describing the Kenyan economy in such metaphorical terms is not mere fantasy. At 'independence' our leaders chose to continue down the path of 'development' laid out by our colonial rulers. As this chapter will demonstrate, such 'development' has been another word for increased economic dependence, and the looting of our national resources. We have long been told that by pulling together and working hard we will soon climb out of poverty. Instead, we find ourselves faced with growing landlessness, unemployment, inflation, shortages of food, and hopelessness.

The great majority of our people live and toil on the land in the rural areas. The wealth produced by them is taken by road and rail to the city. Nairobi is a collecting point founded by the colonialists and developed by international capital for the wholesale export of our produce and our wealth to the dealers of Hamburg, London, and New York. Our people encounter a barren, wasted landscape: a life of stagnation and impotence. Everything of value is extracted for the use of others elsewhere.

With the dismal exceptions of Ian Smith's then Rhodesia, and apartheid South Africa, the gap between rich and poor nearly two decades after 'independence' is wider in Kenya than almost anywhere else in Africa. As we saw in the last chapter, *continuity* was ensured at 'independence'. Continuity meant the wholesale adoption by the KANU government of the inequality underlying the colonial system, when fewer than 4,000 settlers possessed three million hectares of our best land. 'Growth' in colonial and post-colonial Kenya has benefits only for the very few. The attempts of our people to comprehend the reasons for their growing impoverishment have been denounced as anti-*nyayo*, and subversive of peace, love and unity. The survival of our overfed rulers depends on their continuing ability to dupe the people that the State is serving the *national* interest, and that there is only one national interest to be served. The government has, at various times, used the seemingly conflicting ideologies of nationalism and of tribalism to keep Kenyans ignorant of the nature of *class* society which is being formed in their country. *Harambee Nyayoism*, African Socialism all bear the same message: there need be no class struggle in Kenya because Kenyans — true to their mythical African heritage — form one big, united family. There should be no dissension within the family, but all members should obediently follow the lead of the boss who instructs us that what is good for the few is automatically good for all of us.

Ruling class ideology thus projects an imaginary relationship which blurs the real and deep divisions in our society. It aims at preventing our people, or different groups of them, from uniting

to express their own interests. To pretend that classes do not
exist in Kenya is to indulge in fantasy. Of course these classes may
not take the exact form of their Western counterparts. We may
not be able to speak with any precision about a national
bourgeoisie and a landless proletariat in Kenya, since capitalist
development has not taken the same form as that of Nineteenth
Century America and Europe. However, all societies which
produce an economic surplus are class societies, to the extent that
different groups contend over how the surplus is to be produced
and appropriated — and one group dominates the others. In Kenya,
peasants and workers on estates and in towns produce the surplus
which is then appropriated by a capitalist bourgeoisie, both
domestic and foreign.

What, then, is the nature of class society in Kenya? How can we
describe the ruling interest groups, and the use they make of the
State? To what extent is Kenya's domestic bourgeoisie a
dependent class — a mere auxiliary of the foreign capitalist
bourgeoisie? How do the ruling groups exploit the people and
resources of our country: are they productive capitalists or merely
looters of our nation's wealth?

Origins of the Petit-Bourgeoisie

To understand the nature of capitalist exploitation in Kenya and
the origins of our post-colonial ruling class, it is necessary again to
look back at the colonial period. Among some of our peoples,
socio-economic (i.e. class) differentiation was occurring before
direct colonial take-over. Colonialism, which brought Kenyans
into production for the world capitalist market, reinforced and
accelerated this differentiation. Under British rule, pre-capitalist
modes of production were gradually subordinated to the capitalist
mode. This process had, it must be admitted, many desirable and
economically progressive features. It introduced Kenyans to new
resources and instruments of production, and in general raised the
productivity of their labour power. Kenyans were soon producing
a surplus, most of which was appropriated by the colonialists.
Most, but not all. From a very early stage some Kenyans emerged
as petty capitalists, although racist barriers prevented them from
becoming a competitive threat. Thus, by 1915 there were African-
owned and run businesses in Kiambu. By the 1920s, when half
the able-bodied male Luo and Kikuyu were forced into some kind

of 'wage employment', we see signs of an emerging African *petit-bourgeoisie* of shopkeepers, skilled workers, government clerks, teachers etc., a group with access to higher incomes than most of their countrymen. In some cases these Africans were in a position to accumulate a little surplus because of the way *pre*-colonial socio-economic differentiation had whetted their appetite for gain. At colonial take-over they were on the look-out for opportunities to continue the process of self-enrichment, and were willing to collaborate with the colonialists as chiefs and headmen and, in some instances get substantial rewards for doing so. Other members of the embryonic *petit-bourgeoisie* were educated missionary converts, who received relatively large incomes for their work as clerks and teachers — incomes which they could then put to work for them on the land or in small businesses. Those with substantial land holdings could grow cash-crops, like wattle or tobacco. They were not allowed to compete with settler farmers by growing the really lucrative crops, like coffee. African businessmen were severely restricted in their enterprises by the licensing system, which favoured Europeans and Asians, and by their failure to secure credit. But, nevertheless, using the Local Native Councils as a source of loans, capital, and paid employment, they continued to accumulate and invest throughout the colonial period, demonstrating considerable resourcefulness and determination to take advantage of whatever the system had to offer. They displayed a commendable initiative, and refusal to embrace racist propaganda concerning African capacities and their 'proper place' — perpetual servitude.

During the changing international climate of the 1950s, the Kenyan *petit-bourgeoisie* were split in their strategy of how best to advance their interests. Some of its members embraced militant nationalism, seeing the Mau Mau movement as a way of ending the domination of the settlers and opening further avenues to African accumulation. Not all Mau Mau leaders and supporters were acting purely out of self-interest, of course. Some leaders were determined to shed their *petit-bourgeois* outlook, and work for the welfare of all Kenyans and the creation of a truly independent nation. These freedom fighters were regarded as traitors, as renegades, by the large group which saw immediate personal benefit in collaboration with the colonial government in putting down the revolt. These loyalists saw eye to eye with the colonialists on many matters, and fully accepted the idea that progress was only possible for Africans *within* the existing economic framework. They became the apprentice-proteges of colonial and international capitalists, anxious to groom a future ruling class to whom power could safely be entrusted.

A *petit-bourgeoisie* is, in historical terms, a group with interests which straddle the spheres of production and of circulation. Members of the *petit-bourgeoisie may* produce commodities. They may be craftsmen, or artisans, or have other small productive businesses, and at the same time they may be involved in distribution or trade (circulation). Their different interests make them a politically unstable group, with a tendency to frequently switch the alliances they form to further those interests.

In the case of the Kenyan *petit-bourgeoisie*, there was, not surprisingly, little evidence of group unity as the country moved towards nominal independence. But within *petit-bourgeois* ranks, the loyalists were coming into their own. Trusted by the colonial rulers, loyalists were well-placed to take advantage of the opportunities which came their way when international capital deserted the settlers because they were not efficient enough at exploiting the resources of the country. Under the Swynnerton Plan these 'safe' Kenyans were pushed forward by the colonialists to produce cash-crops for the capitalist market, using the profits to consolidate their business interests. African businesses had long been starved of credit, since the Credit to Natives Ordinance of 1926 had restricted to shs.200 the amount which a non-African could lend to an African. This Act was not abolished until 1960. However, in the mid- and late 1950s exemptions were given by the government to those Africans whom it wished to groom for leadership. Various loan schemes, with colonial and American backing, were floated to provide grants to favoured traders. By the end of the 1950s, although African businessmen were still subordinate to European and Asian trading companies, they had carved out a profitable role for themselves as middlemen within the 'reserves'. Furthermore, they were proving themselves to be good future ruling class material. They were eager to embrace the colonial British outlook and style of life, and be embraced in turn as political partners in ruling Kenya. As we saw in Chapter 1, they fully accepted the imperialist version of how 'development' could be achieved in post-colonial Kenya.

The lack of group unity among the ranks of the *petit-bourgeoisie* showed itself clearly in the years after 'independence'. Some *petit-bourgeois* politicians were strongly convinced that Kenya's new rulers had bartered away real independence — these were to follow

Odinga into the KPU. Others, eager to take advantage of the new potential for accumulation offered by control of the state, were determined to bury old differences, saying that in fact *everyone* fought for independence. They were anxious to get ahead in any way they could. Of course, for the majority there were no great rewards — they remained on the outside as small-time shopkeepers, *matatu* owners or distributors. Some individuals within the *petit-bourgeois* ranks did achieve swift upward mobility, thanks to the political alliances which they were able to form. These political and business 'bosses' utilized the State machine and relationships with foreign capitalists to consolidate their uncertain economic base, and emerge as a 'dependent' national bourgeoisie.

Thwarting the Asian Bourgeoisie

Before discussing the national bourgeoisie in more detail, a few words should be said about the Asian business community, which certainly had the potential to become a substantial national bourgeoisie, but for obvious political reasons, failed to do so. During the colonial period, Asians were not allowed to buy land in the so-called 'White Highlands'. They could — and did — take over land in some outlying areas, including western Kenya, where they set up large sugar plantations. But in general, they were blocked from the most productive land, and also blocked from the lucrative import-export business, which remained in European hands. Before World War II the retail trade was the primary outlet for Asian capital. Relying on the closely knit family firm, Asian businessmen were able to spread their trading operations into all the towns of Kenya.

After the war they began increasingly to move into *productive* industry. A few large-scale industrial firms began to emerge, belonging to families like the Chandarias, the Khimasias, and the Madhvanis. These firms produced steel, aluminium, textiles, glass, flour, and molasses. They took over many local companies operating in industry and investment. But in spite of their obvious efficiency and business acumen, the large Asian businessmen have never felt politically secure, and instead of using their profits to consolidate their economic base in 'independent' Kenya, have instead looked for ways to get their capital out of the country. Some have managed to buy a reasonable degree of security and a spectacular degree of wealth by adapting themselves to the new situation and forming partnerships with influential members of the African bourgeoisie, or by acting behind African 'fronts'. The small Asian businessmen have had more reason to feel insecure. From the late 1960s their trading enterprises have been at risk, as the government sought to assure itself of African *petit-bourgeois* support by moving against the Asian business community. In 1967, the Trades Licensing Act excluded non-citizens from trading in rural and outlying urban areas. In the same year, the Kenya National Trading Corporation began to use its licensing powers to force Asians out of the wholesale and retail trade. From 1972 to 1975, many non-citizen *and* citizen Asian businesses were issued with quit notices, and forced to sell to certain well-connected Africans. Again, in late 1980, the Ministry of Commerce attempted in a muddled fashion to enable well-placed Africans to accumulate at the expense of Asians by decreeing that only Africans could operate in combined wholesale and retail spheres, a decision which it was later forced to withdraw. But meanwhile, Asian traders found themselves excluded from trading in some parts of the country and in some commodities. The uncertainty of their position seems to have little to do with their citizenship status.

Nyang'au at the Door

The post-colonial State, therefore, predictably threw its weight against the emergence of the Asian business and industrial community as an indigenous national bourgeoisie. It preferred gradually to foster the interests of a group of African capitalists who were able to use a wide variety of means — legal and illegal — to consolidate their economic base. In many studies of class formation in Africa, post-colonial rulers are characterized as belonging to a *petit-bourgeois* stratum because they rarely produce *value*, but accumulate instead, by acting as middlemen in trade and creaming off profits as goods circulate, or by using their positions in government. Although this has in general been true of the Kenyan ruling class, we choose the term 'dependent' national bourgeoisie for several reasons. For one thing, some of its members have, since the mid-1970s, shown an interest in supplementing the quick speculative return to be obtained in property, business, finance and theft, with a tentative move into production — the Tiger Shoe Company and Madhupaper being two recent examples. But at this stage too much significance can be given to African industrial or productive activity, the success of which is limited by lack of experience, and by extreme dependence on foreign technology and skill and the inclination of the state to suppress foreign competition.

It is important, then, not to over-rate the *productive* nature of the type of bourgeois stratum emerging in Kenya. Its members remain for the most part speculators or looters, not producers. (See Appendix 2–9.) But they qualify as a kind of bourgeoisie because their looting has brought them the ownership of a considerable part of the means of production — in particular, property and land. Like the settlers before them, great tracts of land in their hands are under-used, or left idle. Productivity has declined sharply. They prefer to focus their attention on other enterprises with a quick effortless return. Thus they accumulate through property speculation, through their control of parastatal bodies and marketing boards, through their political roles and positions within the civil service and administration, through the 'sleeping' partnerships they form with Asian businessmen, and — most importantly — through their involvement with foreign capitalists. Multinational corporations give influential Kenyans the opportunity to draw high salaries, sit idly but profitably on boards of directors, own shares, and take part in lucrative sub-contracting ventures. In return, Kenyan directors and allies ensure that multinationals will be able to operate without undue government interference, and will enjoy a certain privileged, near monopoly status in their undertakings. Both sides reap great advantages from their association. For this reason the stratum which provides a favourable political climate for foreign investment cannot be merely termed comprador. The relationship which these influential Kenyans enter into with foreign capital is not completely one-sided, nor does it represent the sum of their activities. Building on a comprador role, they often start and manage their own firms. Holding in some cases 20 or 30 directorships because of the political influence which they are able to command, individuals within this ruling class can accumulate from a wide variety of sources on a scale never dreamed of by their *petit-bourgeois* fathers. But they are hardly more secure, since their extravagant income generally depends on political alignments. Thus, a man like Udi Gecaga, son-in-law of the former President, in the mid 1970s was chairman of the massive Lonrho company in Kenya, a position which he lost in February 1981 since he was no longer politically useful under the new regime. He also had a total of 38 directorships before his fall from political favour. He personally owned seven of these firms, including investment companies, an import company, a transport business, and some trading companies. He has invested extensively in land, both in Kenya and abroad. More of an entrepreneur in his own right than a comprador, Gecaga cannot easily be included in the same class category as the struggling businessman in the rural areas, whose shop might sell five or six commodities, or as the rural schoolmaster who has invested part of his salary in a *matatu*.

Therefore, in Kenya it is useful to distinguish between the *petit-bourgeoisie* and a developing national bourgeoisie with comprador tendencies. Because rich and politically influential Africans have no nation-wide base in production — because productive industrial capital in Kenya is largely in foreign hands — they remain part of an essentially 'dependent' bourgeoisie, a group which is consolidating its base as the *clients* of international capital. Local and international capitalists co-operate to siphon off the surplus produced by Kenyans. But the partnership between them is not one of equals. Local capitalists remain dependent on foreign companies and foreign banks. Their consumption patterns and style of life rely on goods, services and ideas supplied by foreign businesses. Their position remains a precarious one, dependent on the continued willingness of foreign capital to use Nairobi as the base for Eastern African operations.

The Kenyan ruling class and agents of international capital, therefore, derive certain benefits from their association with each other. But it should not be thought that the relationship between them is always happy and conflict-free. Generally, the benefits of co-operation outweigh the disadvantages, but not always. Local capitalists frequently find that their interests might directly compete with those of foreign firms, forcing the state to mediate between them through its licensing procedures and tariff system. But prolonged conflict is unlikely, since neither the government nor the Kenyan bourgeoisie could afford to face the consequences of alienating foreign capital. The government openly states that foreign firms cannot be controlled by the State, and that they drain away huge profits at our expense — but still they are 'vital for development'. Kenya's indigenous firms have to be prepared to play second fiddle, or be taken over by outsiders. Usually a compromise between foreign and national capital is reached, giving foreign firms the dominant market position, while local capital operates on the periphery. Since the rivalry between the capitals is hardly one of equals, local capitalists have been in no position to

45

complain too loudly. For instance, in the case of African-owned
Tiger Shoes, set up in 1972 by the GEMA chief Njenga Karume
and five African ex-managers of the foreign multinational monopoly, the Bata Shoe Company, the annual output of 260,000 a
year is scarcely a threat to the Bata Shoe Company which, in the
middle of the 1970s, produced over eight million shoes a year.
Tiger Shoes can hardly challenge the Czechoslovakian company,
either in its marketing or its advertising. It poses no real threat
to Bata command of the Kenyan market, and its existence can,
therefore, be tolerated.

The Kenya Industrial Estates represent the government's attempt
to promote simultaneously foreign and local enterprise. In this
scheme it is obvious that small-scale African undertakings have been
pushed to the periphery, where they are generally doomed to failure
by a combination of high import content, low level of skills, loan
defaulting, the production of shoddy merchandise, and the inability
to capture markets. For example, such companies as Haraka Hosiery
typically complain that smuggled foreign imports have ruined the
demand for their products. In no way then, does this style of low-
level technology enterprise challenge foreign dominance. Neither
does it provide much in the way of employment. Slightly more
than 1,000 people were working in the Kenya Industrial Estates
in Nairobi in 1980 — far fewer in outlying towns.

We can conclude, then, that given the present economic structure
there is little chance that indigenous enterprise will become
competitive with large international companies which have a
strangle-hold on the Kenyan economy. From the passage of the
Foreign Investment Protection Act of 1964, which allowed those
investors who intended to start businesses 'of benefit' to Kenya
favourable terms on the repatriation of profits and loans, to the
President's recent assurances to the foreign business community
in 1981 that, in the future, they will be able to export even
greater amounts of their capital, the government has sought to
appease — not control — foreign companies. Many members of the
national bourgeoisie have, of course, been beneficiaries of this
unequal relationship. But others, with the *petit-bourgeoisie*,
clearly feel frustrated about the extent of foreign domination in
the country. They would like the government to make a few concrete gestures in the direction of economic nationalism in order to
help them compete. For instance, the Tiger Shoe Company, pushed
out of the low-cost market by Bata's superior rate of production,
has demanded a total import ban on foreign-made shoes in order

to capture the small local market for expensive leather shoes. The government has as yet failed to respond to this pressure, since too many influential trading interests are at stake.

As competition among different groups of the bourgeoisie — national and foreign — for increasingly scarce national resources becomes more fierce, it is possible that resentment over the largely auxiliary role played by the national bourgeoisie may grow stronger and ultimately pose a threat to the security of foreign capital in Kenya. But there is little sign of that happening as yet, perhaps because there are still opportunities for accumulation through the manipulation of government agencies like marketing and licensing boards, co-operatives, land companies, welfare associations, city councils, and through such activities as smuggling and extortion. (See Appendix, especially 2 and 4-7.) As long as a well-placed member of the Kenyan bourgeoisie can pick up the telephone and make himself a handsome cut by ordering the Kenya Meat Commission to provide so many tons of meat to be smuggled into, say, Uganda, he will not have a pressing incentive to engage in directly *productive* business enterprise.

Like cruising sharks, the 'big fish' swim into every nook and cranny of the Kenyan economy, gulping down everything of value, giving little in return. They are able to eat away at the economy at will, forming dubious 'conduit' companies to sidestep tendering systems and siphon off national wealth. They are also able to use their access to the State, and their position as privileged insiders, to purchase from abroad unsuitable or faulty goods, which have turned the economy into a dumping ground for foreign junk. Because of the general abdication of responsibility at the highest levels, these predators are rarely brought to account for their activities. In a system in which the President must personally get his commission — a reported shs. 50 million in the case of the new Nairobi airport — before a major project can proceed, it is hardly surprising that kick-backs, graft and conflict of interests are evident at all levels. Looting brings immediate rewards for relatively little effort, and since the bourgeoisie control the state it entails relatively little risk.

The Foreign Connection

Productive enterprise in the modern economic sector — industry and manufacturing — remains firmly in foreign hands. The pattern of industrial development in Kenya was laid down by the late 1950s; there again, as in land policy, the new African rulers elected to stress continuity, not change. By the late 1950s, Kenya had become the leading industrial centre for the East African market, with a comparatively sophisticated infrastructure of roads, ports, banks and offices being built to superintend the outflow of profits and capital. In 1959, the colonial government showed its determination to attract foreign and British capital by erecting a high tariff which would offer protection to 'infant' industries, including those offspring of multinational corporations. Kenya has never had much in the way of natural resources or minerals to attract foreign interest. What it did, and still does offer, is a favourable government policy towards protection and the repatriation of wealth. What it no longer offers is the gateway to the potentially large East African market, since the forced demise of the East African Community in 1977, and the subsequent border closure with Tanzania, as well as continued chaos in Uganda and long-term hosility to Somalia, have put Kenya in an isolated position in the region. There are signs that, under these circumstances, multinational corporations are beginning to think twice about maintaining their regional headquarters in Nairobi, which is expensive and unrewarding in market terms.

If large foreign firms do pull out of Nairobi in increasing numbers — and the process is beginning — they will leave satisfied, aware that they have for decades extracted super-profits from Kenya, and that the country has little left to surrender. The government has exerted little control over the means possessed by these giant companies to drain away our national wealth. Kenya's is a monopoly economy, dominated by more than 125 American conglomerates as well as large British, West German, Japanese and Scandinavian companies. Large foreign companies have, in many areas — including steel, paint, oil, and metal containers — come to agreements among themselves to fix prices and divide up the market. In other cases (Firestone Tyre Company being an outstanding example) a foreign company has long enjoyed an actual monopoly, with competition being legally barred. (See Appendix 3.)

Once established behind the wall of government protection, foreign companies have opened a door in that wall for the continual outflow of large surplusses. They have, with very little government restriction, repatriated their dividends and profits (created in some cases from *domestic* borrowing, to take advantage of favourable interest rates offered by local banks), and they have used various other techniques to hoodwink the host country concerning the amount of capital being exported. They are the masters of the tax dodge, employing shoals of accountants to help protect their returns from the government tax-man. Their accountants are well versed in such tactics as transfer-pricing, over-invoicing, and double-ledgering to disguise as legitimate payment what is actually another way to repatriate capital. The Nairobi Hilton Hotel, for example, can very well equip the interior of its rooms with locally-purchased fittings. But instead it orders all internal fittings and equipment — its bed linen, curtains, cooking equipment, etc. — from the Hilton chain at high prices, enabling it to transfer out profits in the form of a payment to the parent company abroad.

But Kenya is not, of course, the only victim of the multinational hunt for super-profits. Even in countries in which the government does attempt to act as a watch-dog on multinational corporation activity and stem the drainage of national resources, large foreign firms generally remain one step ahead. Through the sophistication of their accounting systems and their control of technology, they manage to keep the upper hand in negotiations with host governments, and keep profits flowing out. A monster company like Unilever has an annual budget larger than the combined budgets of a group of ten or more African countries — there is absolutely no way the host can possibly control the behaviour of such a robust guest. In the case of Kenya, there is no indication that the government is *trying* to impose restraint on the behaviour of foreign investors. Instead, its overall policy is designed to lure them in, and — as an incentive — let them take out profits, loans, and the interest on loans, royalties, and technical fees, promising meanwhile that they would never be subjected to the indignity of compulsory take-over. Foreign firms are welcomed with open arms to milk the economy of Kenya, in the name of 'national development'.

The Folly of Import-Substitution

Such 'development' has produced a lopsided economic structure, which does little to meet the needs of the people, either their employment needs or needs as consumers. Of course the intention in unrealistic government development plans has been stated in quite different terms. According to planners in the 1960s, Kenya needed foreign-owned import-substitution industry to enable its people to get access to certain manufactured necessities and luxuries. Such industry, it was maintained, would provide large numbers of Kenyans with employment and stimulate indigenous industrial take-off.

Foreign companies were therefore, invited in to produce commodities which had previously been imported, or to put the 'finishing touch' to commodities imported in an unfinished state. As people, including the planners, are now beginning to realize, import-substitution industry in Kenya has been something of an expensive folly. Industries, as we have seen, have been able to take advantage of government licensing and tariff restrictions to set up virtual monopolies. They control the prices. They meanwhile import all their machinery and raw materials, as well as management, and end up producing a product which is *more* costly than the same product would be if imported from abroad. Thus, Kenya at present has three vehicle assembly plants, even though it is uneconomic to produce cars and trucks on such a limited scale. Prices for these vehicles are very high to compensate for the limited market. It would be far cheaper to buy abroad and ship cars to Kenya. Furthermore, import-substitution firms are generally low on quality, and therefore have little export potential. They are notorious for their inefficiency and their shoddy output, since they are allowed to operate virtually free of competition. Union Carbide dry cells leak, K.J. Industries engine oil filters ruin engines; Nalin screws and nails can neither be screwed in nor pounded; Firestone tyres wear out early and rupture at high speeds.

The textile industry provides many illustrations of the syndrome of high prices and low quality which afflicts the entire manufacturing sector. The Rivatex factory at Eldoret has received generous government protection through a high customs duty on imported material and clothes. However, in 1977 the Ministry of Health admitted to importing shs. 3 million worth of nurses' uniforms material because the Rivatex material almost immediately lost its shape, faded, and was easily torn. Besides, the better imported cloth was one-third the price of its Rivatex equivalent. While European countries in the Nineteenth Century made the textile industry the basis of their industrial revolutions, since textiles were a necessity and could find a large domestic market, the Kenyan government seems unaware that textiles can help generate internal economic growth. With a steady need to clothe its institutions and armed forces — one which can be the foundation of a national industry supplying a predictable demand — the government protects Rivatex, allows it to turn out sub-standard cloth, and continues to import uniforms from abroad. (See Appendix 3.) At a very great cost to the whole economy, manufacturing at present produces only about 13% of the national product in the monetary sector. Few of its commodities can be said to be of essential use and benefit to our people as a whole. Import-substitution industry in general panders to the consumption tastes of a small section of our people. However, even members of the national bourgeoisie would, in many cases, prefer to pay high import duties for something of quality or buy illegally-imported foreign goods. Import-substitution industry does *nothing* towards the development of a Kenyan capital goods industry which is necessary if we are ever to move towards self-sufficiency. Instead, it increases our reliance on such expensive in-puts as sophisticated machinery and chemicals, and causes a grave foreign exchange problem, as the government is forced into heavy borrowing in order to afford the imports for the 'modern sector'.

Our country pays in other ways for its 'open door' policy toward foreign investment. Kenya has often found itself landed with sub-standard goods and equipment, and local businessmen or government officials have received generous kick-backs for negotiating such deals. The scandalous rackets in drugs and pesticides are but two of the ways the well-placed crooks in our country have endangered the health and livelihood of the people. Occasionally, foreign investors might themselves prove to be the victims of internal fiddling by the Kenyan bourgeoisie, as is demonstrated by the notorious case of the Ken-Ren fertilizer company at Mombasa. This American-Kenyan joint enterprise was killed by its own Kenyan directors who wanted to continue their lucrative fertilizer import contracts. The collapse of the company swallowed up shs. 70 million of government money, and starved Kenyan agriculture of an essential in-put which is in dangerously scarce supply around the world. (See Appendix 4.)

Other attempts by the government to use foreign industry to stimulate local investment and participation have generally done little more than play into the hands of foreign investors. Government finance has usually resulted in the further squandering of our national resources. Through such agencies as the Industrial and Commercial Development Corporation (ICDC), and the Development Finance Company of Kenya (DFCK), the government has, incredible as it might seem, provided giant multinationals like Unilever, Brooke Bond, and Union Carbide with local resources, and predictably, has got little in way of active control over decision-making in return. It might well be asked what business the government has investing in multinationals, or in certain expensive prestige projects which will do little to stimulate our economic growth. The new Kenya Chemical and Food Corporation in Kisumu, 51% government-owned, is a good example of insanely high investment for dubious returns. Here the government has involved itself with the Madhvani and Mehta companies in one of the most ill-conceived and expensive agro-industrial projects in Africa. During the building phase the project has more than doubled its cost, to a staggering shs. 1,000 million — ten times the original estimate! At the time of writing shs. 200 million of additional revenue has to be found if the project is to be completed, and there is a distinct possibility that the entire undertaking will be abandoned. If this plant ever opens, it will convert molasses into power alcohol at an estimated cost of three times the current world price of petrol, and it will also provide Kenyans with much needed yeast and vinegar. This enormous white elephant will provide only about 600 jobs.

What about the issue of employment? Does foreign-dominated manufacturing — while producing shoddy and expensive goods for a tiny percentage of the Kenyan people — at least supply our people with jobs? According to the statistics, industry in Kenya does not do much in the way of absorbing excess labour. In 1970, employment in the manufacturing sector was a mere 8% higher than it was in 1955, thanks to new capital-intensive technology. In December 1980, manufacturing produced only 14% of the jobs in the modern sector, and this represented a mere 3% of the total number of jobs. In fact, the average annual growth rate of industrial employment may not be more than 1% since 1960. Such employment does not necessarily provide many people with skills, since many of them find jobs in industry only as poorly-paid casual labour.

We can conclude that foreign-owned industry has done little to expand our exports or our employment. Furthermore, the system itself is not internally-expanding as was industrial capitalism in Nineteenth Century Europe. There is little incentive in Kenya for foreign capitalists, whether in manufacturing, finance, or primary commodity production, to reinvest when they can easily repatriate capital, including domestic capital borrowed at low rates from local banks. It is in the interest of foreign firms to consolidate and export their super-profits while the political atmosphere permits them to do so. It is likewise in the interest of those Kenyans with a stake in the system — the Kenyan bourgeoisie — whose members sit on boards of companies and help them get licenses to import costly raw materials, to ensure that the political atmosphere allows a flight of capital out of the country. The government maintains its 'open door' policy, turning our economy into a kind of transit lounge for the comfort of fly-by-night capitalists. To counteract the outflow of capital the government begs loudly for more foreign investment, foreign loans, and foreign 'aid'. It faces a chronic, increasingly grave balance of payments crisis, and comes to rely more and more on the advice and support of the IMF and the World Bank. Our economy is mortgaged to foreign interests, and our people — the producers of wealth which others appropriate — are squeezed further to service the debt and keep the foreigners in business.

What then are the economic prospects facing those who produce the surplusses siphoned off through the State and by the agents of international capital? What does 'development' mean to them?

The Landed and the Landless

Over 90% of our people still live on the land. Many of them face arid, inhospitable conditions, and periodically watch their crops and livestock die for lack of sufficient rainfall. Every few years large numbers of our people face famine, and the usual government response is to deny that famine exists in Kenya.

Only 7% of the land in Kenya has been described as being of high cash-crop potential, with favourable rainfall, soil, and topographical conditions. During the colonial period, most of that land was in the hands of 4,000 settlers, who had more than three million hectares of land with reliable rainfall. Today, much of that high potential land is in the hands of large farmers who, with the land, have purchased the settler vision of the 'good life'. Large farms confer status: status is far more important to these 'telephone farmers' than productivity. In many cases they live in Nairobi, and are too busy looting in other ways to worry about whether their land is being cultivated efficiently or not. The result is — as in the case of settler farming — that half the land belonging to large mixed farms is lying idle. Still, these farmers have all the economic advantages — access to credit and various in-puts needed to raise productivity given proper attention. But the attention is rarely there.

An even more disastrous misuse of land in high potential areas occurs on the large holdings owned by land companies and co-operatives. These are notorious for the way they provide a steady source of loot for their officers and directors, rarely giving anything resembling a decent living to their members. After waiting for years — perhaps even a decade — to be given plots on company-purchased farms, members all too often find that their savings and deposits have disappeared. Many land companies are totally bogus, simply collecting money to buy a farm which might not even be up for sale. Millions of shillings are confiscated from peasants in this way. They are left with nothing, while the swindlers, thriving in an atmosphere of lack of public account-ability, continue their activities unchecked. Stealing from peasants seems to be almost an honourable vocation in Kenya, judging from the social esteem which these thieves can command, and the way the law and police protect them. (See Appendix 5.)

Finally, a considerable portion of high potential land is foreign-owned. Foreign companies still control thousands of acres of tea, coffee, sugar, sisal, fruit plantations and ranches. The government appears more than willing to continue putting the agricultural resources of Kenya at the service of foreign capital. For instance, it obligingly killed small-holder production of pineapples around Thika in order that the American Del Monte Company could have a monopoly. Later, it negotiated a new deal with Del Monte, promising to exempt the company from whatever change might occur in foreign investment policy during a 25 year period. Commodities produced by foreign capital are intended only for limited internal consumption — land which could be used to feed our people produces strawberries for resident expatriates, members of the Kenyan bourgeoisie with Western tastes, and export. Such delicacies are produced by agricultural workers for whom a cup of tea with sugar is a luxury. In May 1980 wages for such workers were pegged at the derisory sum of shs. 215 a *month*, the price of five kilos of coffee in the Nairobi shops.

Tea pickers and sisal workers are generally landless, and hence forced to sell their labour to foreign capitalists. But in the 1950s, international capitalism had recognized that the creation of such a labour force by the wholesale expropriation of peasants from the land was not necessarily a desirable development. Out-and-out proletarianization and landlessness could lead to dangerous political consequences. Besides, if a peasant retained access to some land he could produce his own means of subsistence, and thus subsidize the cost of producing for the capitalist market. A peasant tied to his own individual land-holding would also be less likely to organize politically with his fellow peasants against exploitation. Therefore, for a number of reasons, expropriation of peasants in Kenya has been only partially accomplished. Peasants with small-holdings are regarded by the State and international bourgeoisie alike as a source of cheap labour for the production of commodities for Western markets. In the mid-1970s about 50% of marketed and exported produce was cultivated by these small-scale farmers who have been forced by the need to find money for school fees and other necessities to grow cash-crops instead of food.

In the early 1970s the ILO Report divided Kenya's farming population into three categories: 22% were landless; 44% were small-holders with less than seven acres on which to grow crops for their own use and for sale. Most of these farmers earn the equivalent of less than £60 a year and face a hopeless future on tiny plots which are becoming increasingly overcrowded and impossible to sub-divide in an economic way among children with no alternative means of getting a livelihood. These small-holders have little access to extension services or in-puts like fertilizer and improved seed which might enable them to raise productivity. They can do nothing but hope for a good rainfall and watch land conditions deteriorate year by year. Still, in comparison with the hundreds of thousands of landless, who subsist by squatting, working for others, or begging they (if not their children) are the more fortunate ones, who have access to *some* land and security.

The remaining third of the small-holders have relatively more hopeful prospects, in theory anyway. They own seven acres or more, and are in the position to produce commodities for local sale or export which *should* bring them about £100 a year. But, recently at any rate, they have rarely received their due. In many cases they are at the mercy of marketing co-operatives, which take their crops (co-operatives in the 1970s marketed more than half of all coffee, 40% of all milk, and the entire pyrethrum output) and pay them either a tiny percentage of the final price the commodity will fetch on the market — or, as is the recent trend, don't pay them at all. Farmers can only hope to obtain a fraction of the value of their produce after numerous cuts are taken by unproductive middlemen. Peasant producers are totally subordinated to the vagaries of international commodity quotas and prices over which they exercise absolutely no control, and inefficient, corrupt marketing structures. The quota system might mean that a considerable portion of a cash-crop cannot find its way onto the

market, but will have to be stored. Unfortunately, most
co-operatives and marketing boards have insufficient storage
facilities and refuse to pay for stored produce. The peasants,
therefore, often have little incentive to harvest their crops, which
often rot on ground that could have been put to better use in
essential food production and income generation.

The Coffee Fiasco

In the case of Kenya's leading export commodity — coffee — the
international quota system, lack of local storage, and dumping in
Kenya of sub-standard agro-chemicals, combine to impoverish and
demoralize the peasant farmer. In 1981, farmers lost millions of
shillings because of coffee disease, having been supplied with fake
chemicals sold as coffee fungicides. Even if the crop survives
international racketeering in chemicals, however, it could bring
farmers little income. In 1981, the original quota given to Kenya
coffee, of 78,000 tons, was reduced to 70,000. The reduction was
caused by the fact that year after year the Coffee Board of Kenya
failed to meet its allotted export quota. Instead, Board management in collusion with government officials sold premium quota
coffee very cheaply to bogus non-quota companies owned by
influential people. The 'companies' would then sell off their
coffee in the quota market, making millions for the board
management and their accomplices and political protectors.
Expected production, in 1981-82, of 90,000 tons will be little
short of disaster, since the Kenya Planters Co-operative Union is
in no position to handle and store the glut, and a higher quota
will not be forthcoming. Coffee farmers, who have still not been
paid for the years 1979-80, would get nothing for a crop which
KPCU could not immediately sell. But even if the crop *were* to
find its way onto the international market, the farmers might still
get nothing. The money which has recently been exchanged for
the commodity during its sale in London has largely remained
abroad, being deposited by various members of the ruling
bourgeoisie in foreign banks and invested in foreign assets.
According to the records of the Central Bank, export credit for
the 1980 coffee crop to the tune of shs. 300 million has never come
back to Kenya. Our peasants, with their unending labour, have
been underwriting the crippled Kenyan economy since the coffee
boom ended in 1978. What they so laboriously produce, others

simply appropriate.

Coffee speculation and theft have been the way to wealth for many Kenyans in the 1970s. The coffee boom of 1977, caused by war in Angola and frost in Brazil, brought an enormous short-term windfall for the big growers and those who stole the crop from co-operatives and Uganda and smuggled it out of Kenya. Small-holders with an acre or two of coffee also had a prosperous year, when export prices were pushed 300% higher than they had been in 1975.

Some of the benefits of raised international demand for the crop did trickle down to them. However, the semblance of agricultural 'growth' produced by the boom was wholly artificial and accidental and beyond the control of the government. The boom brought some benefits only to certain farmers in certain regions. It hurt the country as a whole by pushing up all prices dramatically, and further enlarging the appetites of ruling class predators.

Commandeering the Surplus

Thus far, we have only mentioned the inefficiency of co-operatives and marketing agencies, which lack adequate storage facilities and therefore only pay farmers — if they pay at all — for what can immediately be sold. Marketing agencies are not only inefficient; they are also in many cases crooked. Co-operative societies, and the various marketing boards inherited from the colonial administration, originally set up to promote settler agriculture at the expense of African production, are tools used by the ruling class to plunder the peasants. The co-operatives are notorious. Annually, the directors of co-operative societies embezzle millions of shillings which should go to members. Members of the Mukurweini Farmers Co-operative, for example, were bled of a reported shs. 54 million by its officials in 1978 alone, which represents more than shs. 3,000 confiscation per member a year! The Meru Central Farmers Co-operative lost shs. 72 million in the period 1978–80. Because of corrupt practices, membership in the Mathira Dairy Co-operative has dropped from 11,754 to 2,000 in the last three years. No milk at all was taken to the local Kenya Co-operative Creameries by the Nyeri Co-operatives in 1980, because members simply dropped out, realizing they would be paid little or nothing for their produce. (See Appendix 6.)

The marketing boards give producers little more in the way of a fair deal. The boards were set up to assure colonial settlers a virtual monopoly at subsidized prices for their produce. Today, too, the boards — like all parastatals — serve the interests of a particular class — the Kenyan bourgeoisie. By inhibiting competition and controlling the movement and marketing of produce, these boards are able to keep prices paid to producers low, and the cut taken by middlemen as well as final prices on the market high. They give our rulers a further opportunity to consolidate their economic base through nominally legal but dubious means. These agencies provide the leading middlemen — and the State — with an important source of revenue through price mark-ups. The difference between the price paid to the producers and the price paid by the consumers, partly funds the extravagant life-style maintained by the ruling bourgeoisie who superintend the activities of the boards. The boards are, in many cases, as inefficient and riddled with corruption as the co-operatives, and due to the 'milking' practices of their managers nearly all are in dire financial straits. The Kenya Co-operative Creameries, the Kenya Meat Commission, and the National Cereals and Produce Board all hover on the verge of bankruptcy, and indulge in practices which inflict considerable damage on the economy of our country. (See Appendix 7.)

As an example, let us look briefly at the recent activities of the National Cereals and Produce Board, a merger of the former Maize and Wheat Boards. The National Cereals and Produce Board has shown in its brief existence little evidence that it is more efficient than its predecessors. It maintains poor storage facilities, expensive middlemen, and a virtual monopoly over the movement of Kenya's staple food — maize — from producer to market. A surplus beyond the country's internal food requirements is bought cheaply by the Board, and, after being processed by middlemen, is sold abroad at a loss. Between February 1978 and July 1979 nearly 200,000 tons of maize were exported at a loss of shs. 165 million. The rest of the surplus was disposed of in 'mysterious' circumstances, leaving the country to face famine in subsequent years. (See Appendix 8.)

Other Boards are equally unaccountable in their dealings. For instance, the Kenya Tea Development Authority (KTDA) was established in 1964 to develop the small-holder tea industry. Members of the KTDA Board have known how to look after themselves, using their position and inside knowledge to set up private tea processing factories and export companies, such as that at Koisigat and Ngorongo. With the parastatal taking over all tea marketing functions in 1977, Board members have been privately trading in the commodities which they are supposed to administer in the national interest. They are, furthermore, able to squeeze small tea producers by insisting on quality controls, as in the sugar industry. Thus while agricultural workers are paid a pittance to produce for foreign firms, and peasants await payment for their commodities, certain individuals with political influence superintend the outflow of national wealth, making personal fortunes in the process.

The same officials who loot the proceeds of peasant labour work hand in hand with politicians to extort money from the people in other ways. A leading method is that of the *Harambee* meeting, where forced collections are made and seldom accounted for. Here, the 'big shots', who have political influence, are able to use the State to plunder the people in the name of 'self-reliance' and 'development'. If our people try to organize in their own interests, or to fight off the predators, they are told that they are engaging in rumour-mongering — *payukaring* — and that all meetings are illegal without a license from the D.C. From time to time, at considerable risk, our people do rebel, and refuse to perform the role expected of them, that of producing cheaply, commodities wanted by the international market. They refuse to harvest tea in Kisii; they burn sugar plantations in the west; they let coffee rot on the bush in Central Province. Such protests are generally smashed by the G.S.U. The only further recourse open to the impoverished small-holders, the landless and their children, is that of migration, or more properly, drift.

According to the government's economic survey for 1980, agricultural production in Kenya must more than *double* in the next 20 years in order to deal with a rate of population increase, which is the highest in the world. There is no sign of the country moving in that direction. Instead, agricultural productivity is *declining* year by year. The government blames drought and the will of God. It chooses to overlook the prolonged demoralization of our people and the massive depletion of national resources which government policies and looting have brought about.

Our land is slowly dying. Our people experience increasing wretchedness and desperation as the only share of growth which our leaders talk so loudly about. Their holdings get smaller as their families get bigger. They can do little to counteract soil exhaustion and erosion, and remain perennially vulnerable to drought and disease. Kenya has become incapable of feeding her people, as

millions of hectares of the best land — in the hands of foreign
owners and the bourgeoisie — are put to exclusive production for
export. Marketing regulations and prices paid to producers
discourage the cultivation of basic food crops. Much food that is
produced often rots on the ground. For the majority of people in
the rural areas, then, the future holds out little hope of a better
standard of living. Those with initiative and maybe some education,
who want something better for themselves and their children than
deteriorating conditions and strangled expectations, are forced to
go to the towns to look for work.

Hakuna Kazi

Those who migrate from the rural areas to the towns do not form
a proletariat in the Nineteenth Century European sense. Peasants
in Nineteenth Century Europe went to look for work in the new
industries of the towns when they were expropriated from the
land. Largely uneducated and illiterate, they were forced to sell
their labour for a wage, having no means of subsistence to fall
back on. Generally, they found a ready market for their labour,
since industry around Europe was swiftly expanding and needing
larger and larger numbers of factory 'hands' to tend newly-installed
machines. In bad times they would be laid off, swelling the ranks
of the unemployed — the 'industrial reserve army' — whose
presence enabled the capitalists to keep wages low and profits
accordingly high.

In Kenya the reservoir of labour — the *kibarua* — is not only
made up of the expropriated and uneducated. Many of our migrants
still have ties with the land but have a certain level of education
which has bred heightened expectations that cannot be satisfied
on the land. Finding nothing but stagnation in the rural areas,
they, in many cases, find nothing awaiting them in the cities.
There are hundreds of thousands of school leavers like themselves
who are hoping to find non-manual employment as the key to
upward mobility. They naturally aspire to enter the ranks of the
petit-bourgeoisie and bourgeoisie. They emulate the civil servants
and government employees who, thanks to the Ndegwa Report of
1971, can hang their coats over their office chairs and go off to
tend their private business interests. Even more enviable are the
really successful ones who form alliances with politicians, get
access to special licensing privileges and council plots, and take

over non-citizen enterprises. These accumulators have been held up as the models for our aspiring youth.

These aspirations cannot be safely ignored by the State, since seeming to satisfy them is the key to political stability. For this reason the State has enormously expanded the civil service, which has doubled in size in the period 1971–80, with over 170,000 now being employed in the administration and various ministries. If teachers are added, the figure increases to over 250,000. There are 50,000 in the high ranks of the bureaucracy. The government has to keep them in their lordly positions, make sure that pay differentials at this level are maintained, and at the same time seek to absorb Sixth Formers and University graduates into the overloaded public sector. But such expansion of the public sector, financed by the surplus produced on the land, cannot go on indefinitely. The 1980 statistics were not encouraging. 1,156,900 people were reported as employed or self-employed in the modern and informal sectors, while a further 260,000 job seekers had, in a few days, registered themselves with the Ministry of Labour. It is unlikely that the unemployed will be found jobs with the State. Neither will they — like their Nineteenth Century European counterparts — be able to find jobs in manufacturing. Since the working population will increase by at least 250,000 a year in the 1980s, the government is facing a grave problem, that of massive unemployment.

As we have seen, industry in Kenya provides relatively few jobs, and is unlikely to change its employment pattern in the future. Capitalism is no longer geared to Nineteenth Century technology. Capital-intensive technology ensures the largest profits. It will not be abandoned because of an unemployment crisis, regardless of the needs of the State.

International capitalism operating in Kenya has an interest, with the State, in forestalling the emergence of a fully-expropriated proletariat. As long as most workers maintain links with the land, possibly in the form of a home plot tilled by the wife who earns family subsistence, firms can pay their workers low wages. Peasants with individual land-holdings, no matter how insufficient, can be more easily divided and controlled than landless labourers. There-fore, both the international and national bourgeoisie have a stake in preventing classes from being fully formed on Western lines. 'Straddling' of classical class categories is common in Kenya and other 'Third World' countries. Thus, we have the situation of the wage worker in the town relying on his wife in the 'reserves' to produce the family subsistence. He feels 'temporary' in the town, and aspires to get back to the land some day. His sense of himself as belonging to an urban working-class is correspondingly weak.

Both the 'modern sector' and the State get certain advantages from the existence of the so-called urban 'informal sector'. Street hawkers, shoeshine boys, small-time mechanics, and producers of cheap furniture, shoes, *jikos*, etc., all work in the informal sector. These are the most exploited of our workers, having to put in long hours under uncontrolled conditions in order to keep themselves alive. Workers in the modern sector, who cannot afford to purchase the items which they manufacture in import-substitution industry, rely on this 'informal sector' for the necessities of life. Big firms can, therefore, keep wages lower than they would otherwise be, since they do not have to afford the worker and his family a living at 'modern sector' prices. Furthermore, the informal sector absorbs some excess labour and, in so doing, contributes to political stability. More than 200,000 people now eke out a living in this way, using great ingenuity and a few basic tools to recycle the garbage of capitalism. They cling to the edges of the cities, hoping to hang on until formal employment is found. Generally that day never comes.

All workers in the towns, those in informal and formal employment, were hard hit during the 1970s by steeply rising prices and rents. The present minimum wage for an unskilled worker in Nairobi — shs. 456 a month — will hardly pay the rent for a room in a shanty. Workers get little assistance from their unions whose leadership has promised to stick to government wage guidelines. The State-controlled umbrella union, COTU, is totally subordinate to the President and his Cabinet who frequently warn its members that strikes are illegal. As far as the expansion of employment is concerned, the future looks grim. A Presidential decree that all employers should increase their labour force by 10% is a desperate remedy which further lowers the productivity of labour. But for the time being, the ominously growing industrial reserve army forces the mass of workers into submissiveness. Workers rarely dare step out of line, fearing that if they lose one job they will never get another. Meanwhile, the population continues to rise. The August 1979 census put the Kenyan population at 40% higher than the census of the previous decade. More than half that population of 15,322,000 are under the age of 15. They will soon be following their parents and elder brothers and sisters and looking for work. Since the rural sector is declining in productivity, the

public sector has reached saturation point, and the manufacturing
sector is contracting with the end of easy import-substitution
'growth', how will they realize their hopes of leading productive
lives? The government has no answer, no plan, no advice except
'go to school, work hard and pray to the Lord'.

The IMF Kiss of 'Life'

Kenya's economic prognosis is hardly encouraging. Inflation in
recent years has led to a sharp decline in real income and a drop in
the standard of living in the towns and rural areas. The government
recently shelved its own unrealistically optimistic *Development
Plan for 1979-83*, and in a subsequent Sessional Paper admitted
that the days of 'soft options' were over, and that Kenya's rate of
growth would continue to decline. The government has been swift
to put the blame on purely external causes — especially on the
effects of international recession, inflation, and rising oil prices, as
well as drought. Of course, there is some truth in this. The price
which Kenya has paid for oil has increased four-fold since 1973.
But it would be wrong to overlook the way our leaders — through
a combination of greed, incompetence, mismanagement, and
criminal short-sightedness — have encouraged our present state of
dependence on external variables, have abetted the draining away
of our national wealth, and through it all have remained politically
unaccountable.

The government has tolerated and even connived at a steady
seepage of national surplus when Kenya needed all her resources
if 'development' was to be more than a hollow word. According to
one estimate, nearly £100 million left our 'independent' country
in one way or another before 1969. After 1969, the outflow became
a flood, and a positive torrent following the assassination of JM
in 1975 and the death of Kenyatta in 1978. Ours has been a
frontier-style economy, where anything goes. During the late 1960s,
the national bourgeoisie discovered easy pickings to be made
through poaching, and the export of ivory. In the mid 1970s,
they looted our nation's mineral wealth and forests, as gemstones
and charcoal were shipped out of the country in great quantities,
and the enormous proceeds deposited abroad. Recently, in the
late 1970s, their search for the quick return took a more ominous
form. While Kenyans face famine, well-connected individuals sell
to neighbouring countries maize and grain purchased at

concessionary prices from America and South Africa. (See Appendix 8.) Such actions on the part of the ruling class seem to indicate little faith in the future of the country.

Indeed, since Kenyatta's death, the soaring flight of capital has made that future even more uncertain. Substantial businessmen — African, Asian, and European — have been repatriating whatever they can lay their hands on. At a time when foreign exchange reserves have been deteriorating rapidly — the December 1980 deficit of £90 million represented a fall of £162 million in a single year — leading members of the government have contributed to driving the country into bankruptcy. Our new rulers, the new order of *nyang'au*, show little sense of self-restraint even for their own survival, and an alarming lack of simple business acumen. With the level of foreign exchange insufficient to cover three months' worth of imports, the President shelled out our money for a new Boeing Jumbo for the virtually bankrupt national airline, pocketing $2½ million in the process. He ordered that his face appear on the national currency, and got another large commission along the way. He has also moved into large-scale property buying, grabbing up such prestigious towers as International House in Nairobi and land in England with nationally-borrowed foreign exchange. Other members of his entourage have also been buying farms and mansions abroad, and depositing huge sums in their Swiss bank accounts.

Given the rate at which its most prominent members continue to repatriate our assets, and invest money abroad, it is hardly surprising that the government has been unable to stabilize the situation by borrowing abroad. Government policy, projected in budgets and development plans, continues to bear little relation to economic reality. The ruling bourgeoisie continues its gross over-indulgence, importing without restriction shs. 600,000 Mercedes Benz, Volvos, and BMWs, while the import of nuts and bolts for productive use is banned on the grounds that it is draining away our foreign exchange. Nairobi supermarkets continue to titillate the tastes of expatriate residents who maintain in our capital city a standard of living considerably higher than that they knew at home. While our country sinks into a quagmire of indebtedness, UNEP-type parasites drink their French wines and eat their Russian caviare, giving our own bourgeoisie an 'international' life-style to emulate. There seems to be no co-ordinated effort on the part of government ministries to curb the bourgeois appetite and safeguard our dwindling reserves by restricting imports to productive essentials.

Instead, the government seems almost totally devoid of any policy direction whatever, blundering from one decision to its opposite. There is routine talk at the highest levels about 'hard options' and 'belt tightening' and in the end nothing is done. At present the country imports approximately twice as much as it exports, a situation which cannot go on indefinitely. Parliament, unlike parliaments elsewhere, has no control over purse-strings, and no ability to induce a note of caution into the government's reckless course. Instead, its Public Accounts Committee is constantly being interfered with by the Office of the President. Under the circumstances, the only remedy which government seems able to utilize is the begging bowl. From 1972, the government has turned more and more often to external borrowing as a way of closing the gap between domestic production and domestic consumption. In 1964, our public debt stood at £86 million, and then began to rise steadily, reaching £160 million in 1970 and nearly £312 million in 1975. The public debt in 1979 stood at nearly £578 million, approximately 10% higher than the debt for 1978. Figures continue their upward spiral, until at present Kenya is one of the world's top borrowers. In order to service its debts and compensate for the bleeding of foreign exchange, the government is forced to seek additional loans from 'friendly' nations, the IMF and the World Bank. In return, it accepts IMF and Bank advice about when to devalue the currency, and what currency restrictions to place on residents — restrictions which have yet to be enforced. In 1980, the Kenyan government got itself out of a potentially disastrous situation by negotiating $30 million food aid from America, and made additional purchases of wheat, maize, rice and milk in 1981 from America, South Africa, Australia and elsewhere. In all, the government spent over shs. 1,000 million for cereal imports in 1980–81. A government forecast, in Sessional Paper No. 4 of 1981, estimated that the import bill for maize alone will be shs. 2,500 million for 1981–83. Kenya's reputation as an international mendicant grows, while hopes for achieving self-sufficiency in food production remain confined to the pages of optimistic economic plans, drawn up to demonstrate our present and future credit-worthiness. The reality is of growing indebtedness and dependence, and reliance on the life support system which will be provided by the IMF and World Bank, as long as we are considered to be 'deserving'.

Why, it might be asked, should they bother to keep us from

complete collapse? What do we have that international capital wants? Kenya, after all, lacks the sort of mineral wealth which has led to the ransacking of a country with vast potential like Zaire and buys support for apartheid South Africa. With the disintegration of the East African Community, and closing of the border with Tanzania, our country can offer little in the way of an extensive regional market, and our own domestic market is small. The only things we can offer international capital are pliant government policy, an implacably 'anti-Communist' official ideology, and a strategic location near the Horn of Africa.

Thus far, the government has been only too eager to follow the marching orders issued by the IMF, and in all likelihood will continue to play the obedient waif in the future. At the request of the IMF and World Bank, it will continue to forbid strikes, and agree to low wages for our workers and an open door for imports and profit repatriation. The President, at the end of 1980, took pains to reassure foreign investors that no matter how dismal Kenya's economic prospects, investors will in the future be able to repatriate capital *with greater ease* than in the past. The government paid for America's maize with bases at Mombasa and elsewhere, for the patrol of the Indian Ocean and Persian Gulf, thereby doing its bit to keep the region 'safe for democracy'. In the future it is likely that we will deepen our crippling dependence on the United States and the industrial West. As long as the government can prove that it is 'worthy' of Western loans and 'aid' — as long as it continues to put the profit margin of international capital before the welfare of its citizens — Kenya will in all probability find a bed waiting for it in the intensive-care ward for subservient Third World client states. In a neighbouring bed, occupied by prostrate, debt-choked Zaire, it will discover the vision of its own plundered future.

4. The Culture of Dependency: *Hakuna Njia Hapa!*

The disease of dependency has poisoned our nation's life-blood. Transfusions from the capitalist West — taking the form of grants, loans, and 'aid' — have, in the short-term, kept our invalid economy from total collapse, but the long-term diagnosis is not encouraging. The government seems deluded as to the nature of the disease, lulled into the belief that IMF's *uchawi* is good for the system, and that the best possible treatment is being obtained. Dependency has become a way of life, and the way to death. Dependency in Kenya is mental as well as material. We have been deprived of the opportunity to *act* and to realize our creative potential as individuals and as a nation. Instead, we are taught to further stifle initiative in ourselves and our children, and told to follow — blindly, mutely, meekly. Our leaders have made themselves mental mendicants, habitually dependent on the outside world for support and direction. This is the path they order us to follow; a path that leads to impotence and national ruin. In order to revive our country and our capacities, we must veer from this hopeless destination and fight for our lives and our future.

In this chapter we will honestly confront the fact of our mental and cultural dependency. We must first be able to recognize the problem — its depth and all-pervasiveness — before seeking solutions to our condition. The roots of the dependency syndrome are embedded in colonial history. Our people were uprooted from their traditions and customs and forcibly enlisted in the army of the Lord. They were taught to believe in their 'innate inferiority', so that they could be more easily manipulated by the ruling 'master-race'. Their confidence and self-reliance were destroyed. They were drilled to obey and to take orders. Colonialism sought to reduce us to perpetual servitude.

As we saw in the first chapter, there was continual resistance to colonial domination. However, 70 years of persistent indoctrination gradually took their toll. By the end of the colonial period a mentally emasculated group had been produced, ready to invite further outside domination. It must be admitted that the loss of the sense of self-direction, and cultural and mental integrity, had pervaded the entire society.

The independence which the nascent ruling class brought back from Lancaster House reflected our wounded national self-image. Proper decolonization — real independence — could only be based on the regeneration of cultural self-confidence, and the creation of a sense of national direction and pride. As we have seen, decolonization has never taken place. We have yet to experience real independence. What we *have* experienced — 20 years of concentrated neo-colonialism — has merely reinforced the dependency syndrome.

We can state unequivocably that 'independence' under KANU has further crippled our faculties. Dependency is now an all-encompassing condition, pervading all spheres of national life: economic, political and cultural. The withering away of KANU, and the war waged against popular participation in the political realm and in economic decision-making, has virtually killed our national self-assertiveness and self-esteem.

Kumtumbuiza Raisi

Under these circumstances, what is left of our culture? We have a Minister of Culture who applauds the dancers at the Bomas of Kenya, as they perform under the eye of their American choreographer. We have groups of tired 'traditional dancers' who wearily go through their paces at State House, praising the king and his court, and being fortunate to get a soda as their reward. We have a so-called Kenya Cultural Centre, leased from the British Council, which caters totally to foreign tastes. In the cultural void foreign houses have moved in to provide entertainment for their nationals, occasionally inviting lecturers from the University to discourse on 'Kenyan Culture'. We have a so-called National Theatre which specializes in bedroom farces, Gilbert and Sullivan, and acts as host to touring musicians from Europe. And in a recent series of stamps, various colonial buildings — including the P.C.'s headquarters, with its strong resemblance to a Victorian public lavatory — have been declared national cultural monuments!

While foreign culture cuts deeply into Nairobi, and feeble imitations of something which was once vital and meaningful to Kenyans pose as our 'rich cultural heritage', the Kamirithu Community Theatre is proscribed and our most distinguished author detained and then forced into seclusion. Surely Kamirithu, tapping the creative energies of our people, and Ngugi-wa-Thiong'o are the carriers and creators of a wholly authentic cultural expression? Can the same be said for the lifeless dance routines displayed to tourists at the Bomas of Kenya?

A national culture is not something static, for display only. It is not a fossilized museum piece. Instead, it must be seen as a dynamic process, involving *people* and their creative capacities. What we call culture is the representation of the meaning and values which people give to their lives and society. It is produced by a complex, reciprocal relationship between the community and its entire environment — physical, social, and political. It is something vital: a living, ever-changing process of self-discovery.

In the absence of anything else, many Kenyans have adopted the more inane aspects of foreign life and thought. Our cultural existence is today imported, like so much else. We mimic images of the outside world. Because of our inability to develop and hold fast to our own cultural moorings, we easily succumb to foreign advertisers and salesmen who swamp us with cultural claptrap and alien values produced by foreign profit-hunters. We succumb because we are surrounded by a void of our rulers' making. In the 20 years of pseudo-independence, society has been fragmented and our creative potential stunted. We have been deprived of what we had under colonial rule — a culture of *resistance*. Fearing that a vital cultural and intellectual life would pose a threat to continued foreign control and their own lofty positions, our rulers have ruthlessly suppressed even the beginnings of local self-expression. They have treated our people like children, saying that they know what is best, and that they will do all our thinking for us. All *we* have to do is obey, and follow. We even need a D.C.'s permit to gather together, to generate new ideas and institutions, and to create something of our own, and that permit is rarely forthcoming.

Our leaders are our bosses. They tell us what to do, and when to do it. The President is, so we are continually told, our 'father', which makes us irresponsible children. An ex-schoolmaster, Moi treats the country like his classroom. By this statement, we do not mean to imply that he actively cultivates *learning*. On the contrary, a classroom situation in Kenya rarely encourages mental growth. That is not its function. Instead, classroom activity is generally organized along rigidly authoritarian lines, designed to kill initiative and independent thought. Thus, in the same way as our children are drilled to chant back answers and never to question, our people are forced to chant their loyalty pledge and are punished if they question matters of policy. Any sign of initiative, any stepping out of line, evokes the threat of the cane, as government doctors recently discovered. This stern headmaster-role adopted by the man at the top can only be carried out if our education system does its job 'properly' — the job of killing the mind, training the voice to produce the 'right' answers, and grooming future rulers to perpetuate the system.

Starving the Mind

Dominant groups in all societies attempt to use education to stablize and reproduce the *status quo*. It is a powerful ideological tool, used to indoctrinate the young with the values and outlook of those who rule. However, instead of instilling conformity, it can, in certain situations, become subversive of that outlook: an example from our colonial past was the 'independent school movement'. For this reason, because education can — if it produces independent thinkers — be used as a weapon *against* rulers, governments which are unsure of the depth of their support among the population do not take chances with the educational system. They seek to control it from above, to tell its teachers what and how to 'teach' and to make certain that the educational system is used to deaden, and not to stimulate, mental growth.

One way to ensure that education does not become a 'subversive' activity is to separate the 'educated' from the 'uneducated' socially, politically, and spiritually. The educated are told that they are members of the elite, set apart from, and above the rest of society. In this way, potential leaders are, so to speak, cordoned off from the rest of the population, and when properly groomed, reimposed on the population to lead in directions already laid down by the ruling class. People are told to educate their children, and then some of their children are turned and used against them.

The missionaries pioneered this approach to education in Kenya. Before they brought the concept of the formal school, to be used to acquire literacy (for Bible reading) and a few other skills required by the colonialists, education among our people was geared to the reproduction of their social and economic needs. It was related to the lives of all the people, not something set apart. Education was socialization.

We should, of course, recognize that literacy and numeracy brought enormous benefits, and enabled our people to attain a wider world outlook. However, from the earliest colonial period the formal school was primarily a vehicle of propaganda and indoctrination, and not of education in its true sense. The colonial education system served to convince the colonized of the virtues and superiority of foreign domination, and to mould a select few to be the petty officials and agents of Christianity and alien rule. Missionary education aimed at uprooting the *asomi* from their communities and traditions, and setting them against their own people's interests. The educated became 'civilised'; those outside the magic circle of the mission station and school remained 'barbaric heathen'.

Under the impact of colonialism, traditional society — with a few isolated exceptions — went the way of traditional education. The imported brand of British-style education served the needs of the colonists, by providing them with literate underlings who accepted and shared the world view of the foreign ruling class. However, missionary education also proved the undoing of the colonial ruling class, since it raised up the nationalists who felt frustrated by continual subordination in their own land. We have, elsewhere, examined the conflicting states of mind of these nationalists, seeing that many of the moderates among them simply wanted the British out in order to step into their shoes, while others wanted a radical change in Kenya and a meaningful independence. We have seen that by 'independence' the moderates defeated the radicals. This defeat was not, however, a foregone conclusion in 1960. The KANU *Manifesto* of that year was a document that sought to rally the support of both radicals and moderates. Its ringing statement on education appears today as a relic of our nearly vanished culture of resistance:

> The children of Kenya must be taught to build their mother-land and to love her rather than be allowed to develop a slavish mentality under a stilted education [system] . . .
> Education should instil the love of one's motherland and way of life. It should train youth to love the freedom of their mind and body . . . foster pride . . . build one's country into a great nation. It is KANU's contention that the present

71

educational system does not make the African student take his rightful place. . . . What we see is the drive among educated people to compete with local Europeans in the superfluities of life.

The 'drive among the educated' to emulate Europeans in the 'superfluities of life' aptly describes the ruling class of today. However, this situation no longer causes concern to KANU. Instead, in the post-colonial period, the party has fully accepted the view that the point of education is to enable *some* Kenyans to imitate and compete with Europeans, to rule over their fellow Kenyans as the British ruled over them. Colonial education has continued virtually unchanged since 'independence'. In the 20 years since its first *Manifesto*, KANU has made no visible move to decolonize the aims and content of the educational system. The government has merely tinkered around with the curricula in schools, and has adopted fully British values and style of education for a subject people. Thus, as in colonial times, the teacher makes pronouncements; the pupils dutifully chant them back unquestioningly and commit them to memory. There is little attempt to teach students to think for themselves, since that is not the point of this type of education. Instead, they must be taught to think what the teacher wants them to think, and to obey. The emphasis, as in former times, is on drill, and the most unimaginative form of rote learning.

The few changes that have been proposed are often mis-conceived, illogical, or even banal. We have yet to see any structured programme designed to carry them out. As far as we know, nothing has been done to implement the Presidential decision making the duration of primary school education nine years and a National Youth Service compulsory after Sixth Form. In these major areas of education, planning seems totally haphazard and devoid of content. The President recently decreed that the New Maths be speedily abolished, on the grounds that it was part of an imperialist plot to keep down Kenyans. The profound way the imperialists exert their influence through the *rest* of the educational system — most of it a good deal more rigid and less imaginative than the New Maths — is totally overlooked. Rather than exposing our youth to new ideas and possibilities, exploring and stimulating their potential, and opening paths to a new *non-colonial* mental landscape in order to decolonize the mind, the education system of 'independent' Kenya has merely reinforced past forms and content.

Ours is still an education designed to produce passivity on the part of the learners, and to dull and repress their initiative.

It is a dismal fact, but one which must be openly confronted, that our mental and cultural life today is nearly as moribund as our economy. Our leaders must be condemned for their collaboration with foreign interests, their greed, and addiction to 'eating'. But they must be damned even more thoroughly for the crimes they have committed against the spirit of our people. In post-colonial Kenya we see little evidence of the 'pride' and 'freedom of mind and body' which fired the hopes of some writers of KANU's first *Manifesto*. We see, on the contrary, plentiful evidence of the 'slavish mentality' developed under an unimaginative stilted education. Present-day Kenya shows little sign of the explosive energy, initiative, creativity and resourcefulness that characterize vital new social formations. But since there is little 'new' about 'independent' Kenya, this is perhaps not surprising.

No Groupings Allowed

But our leaders are not only culpable for their conspicuous failure to generate new levels of productivity and initiative among our people. The truth of the past 20 years is far more bleak. During that time, our leaders have not only failed to stimulate a renewal of spirit and energy among our people, but they have gone out of their way to *destroy* the initiative and creativity which had survived the colonial period. Traditionally, all Kenyan ethnic groups had evolved communal organizations for mutual self-help and communal improvement. These were strengthened during the colonial period, and some of them turned into important instruments of resistance. Significantly, none of these democratic institutions were given new life after 1963. Instead, they were replaced by large centralized bureaucratic bodies which were unresponsive to the people they 'served'. *Harambee* projects and co-operatives became mere vehicles of exploitation, under the control of an oppressive ruling class. The concerted effort by our rulers to disorganize society, to discourage or break up forms of community organization, which had once generated a culture of resistance, serves as an eloquent testimony to the fact that the leaders of this country perceive the mass of our people as potential enemies, to be kept down at all costs. They would happily turn us into a nation of zombies, in order to make their positions secure and place themselves beyond criticism and challenge. Under our present circumstances, *any* communally-based form of self-assertion is a positive development which must be encouraged. Even the so-called 'tribal organizations', recently banned by the government in their efforts to kill GEMA, can fulfil an important social function by bringing people together to express their needs. However, we must recognize that the ruling class has often used these associations for its own devious and collusive purposes. The active promotion of such narrow ethnic organizations can only be recommended in the absence of anything better.

There is at present no clearer illustration of the fear with which the rulers regard the people than the so-called 'philosophy' of *nyayoism*, which seeks to *glorify* passivity — 'follow me, sheep!' Ideology is used by the ruling class to make people passive followers so they will forget their capacity to judge, to initiate, to act. Any rediscovery of these three qualities on the part of an individual or group leads to that individual or group being denounced as anti-*nyayo* and subversive. *Nyayo* followers are properly docile, submissive, and inert. They (in the wishful thinking of the ruling class) can be easily led and induced to produce wealth for others to appropriate.

Campus Farce

The future appropriators are forced to adopt this pernicious ruling class mentality at schools, and have it strengthened at University. The University is the pinnacle of our neo-colonial education system. It essentialy acts as a 'future leaders' cooking-pot, into which are thrust those few bright students who have survived the primary and secondary school exam-sifting process. Unfortunately for the students and our country, the University of Nairobi can hardly be said to function as a proper University. If education through secondary school is irrelevant, expensive and intellectually stultifying, our University provides the same and more. It does little or nothing to promote curiosity and intellectual awareness on the part of the student. There is little discussion about new ideas and their social applicability — in fact, there is little discussion of any sort. If a University should be an institution where all tendencies of thought are presented and allowed to contend, ours certainly does not merit the name. For the last ten years, the ruling authorities, fearful of the influence of 'foreign ideologies', have sought to make the University of Nairobi little more than a costly finishing school; at best a glorified polytechnic, where some skills are mastered but the social context in which the skills are applied is not to be questioned.

The result is a predictable one. The University of Nairobi produces few doctors who are willing to work in the rural areas. They have no interest in creating forms of medical service that suit poor, rural illiterate societies. The same is true of engineers, architects, agriculturalists, and veterinarians who pass through our unreformed educational system. All these graduates are rather expected to learn how to 'climb' and do well for themselves. Aspiring to a privileged life, they are determined to segregate themselves in high-rent districts of towns, and go into some lucrative private business: the welfare of the people is not their concern.

The University thus seldom encourages its students to put their skills to socially-beneficial use. But it fails even more miserably in that area of learning which does not involve the imparting of practical skills — in the humanities, or liberal arts. The humanities involve the study of human thought and economic, social and political structures. Students *should* be able to apply what is relevant in their studies to present problems, engaging in vigorous — even fierce — debate, and ultimately deriving new directions for their own societies and the nation. But University of Nairobi humanities students are not encouraged to study and think in these terms. The ruling class is mortally afraid of discussion and new ideas. It uses its control of the University administration to limit academic debate and suppress discussion. Thus, symposia on national problems are banned by the President in his capacity as Chancellor of the University, unless they are sponsored by imperialist cultural agencies. The Chancellor and his minions virtually decree what is to be taught, and which books are not to be read. They bar students and lecturers from forming extra-curricular associations, from publishing newspapers and magazines, from coming together to discuss or even socialize. They summarily shut the University at will (more frequently as years go by), and manage to reduce it to a wasteful laughing-stock. Over the years, it has become a University in name only, kept going for purposes of national prestige and opportunities presented for looting. (See Appendix 9.)

Students generally leave this dismal institution with little sense of regret. What should have been stimulating years spent pondering

new social and intellectual possibilities and how they could be
adapted to the Kenyan situation, are instead years of uncertainty,
tedium, and more rote learning. If, during those years, students
encountered a single lecturer who made them think about these
issues, they could consider themselves fortunate. Many lecturers
have never addressed their minds to these questions, and the few
that have are under tremendous pressure not to take principled
positions. The University thus reflects the general repression of
thought, initiative, and creativity now endemic in Kenyan society.
The intrigue and factionalism which characterize our society
prevent University teachers and students from taking any type of
unified action or stand.

However, despite government intimidation, there is a growing
rebellion of youth at all levels of the education system. More and
more secondary and University students are showing signs of
rejecting passive, irrelevant learning carried out under drunken or
absent teachers and headmasters. There is ample evidence that
individual students are asserting the right to self-discovery and
self-expression, a development which the government attributes
to 'outside interference' or a spoiled 'disregard of authority'.
Can we see in these widespread student protests and demonstrations
the beginnings of a revolt against the present dead-end colonial
educational diet which might ultimately spell its long-overdue
demise?

Ineptitude Rewarded

For the present, education — such as it is — remains the key to
upward mobility. It provides new recruits for the class that acts
against the interests of the majority of Kenyans. Students are
taught, or forced by default, to aspire for 'something better' than
the life which their parents know. They aspire to join the parasites,
those who produce nothing themselves, but grow fat on the labour
of others. Unfortunately, this outlook is diffused through the
entire society. It is a general assumption that the educated *should*
enjoy a privileged existence, that they *should* be supported in a
lofty manner simply because they have been expensively educated:
'we have educated them, now we must keep them happy'. The fact
that they give practically nothing to society in return — that their
so-called education has left them almost bereft of useful skills
which can be of social service — is only recently being seen as a

problem. What does it matter if the graduate engineer has never got his hands dirty examining an engine or mixing cement? If the colonialists never did physical work, why should the Kenyan replacements who aspire to slot into their roles and achieve their social status? Most 'educated' Kenyans assume that they should be automatically entitled to the 'good life', by which they mean one free of strenuous labour.

The financial and social cost of raising up this 'educated' caste is enormous, and increasing every year. It is clear that our country cannot long afford to nourish and support their aspirations. More than 40% of the budget, as well as *Harambee* contributions, is utilized for pumping out innumerable unemployables. Today, some 10,000 primary schools produce half a million school leavers annually, only a quarter of whom find places in high schools. The rest drop out of the system, too 'educated' for their rural homes and too unskilled for any useful employment. They promptly join the growing heap of jobless from past years. Secondary schools in their turn now annually turn out 50,000 school leavers who have completed their course, who join their predecessors in the queue of millions looking for some form of employment. It has been estimated that since 1960 nearly six million C.P.E. and E.A.C.E. candidates could be classified as unemployed. Now the same phenomenon is beginning to occur with University graduates. These are the expensive products of an unreformed, overloaded education system which can no longer serve effectively to provide a ladder for the socially ambitious.

We do not mean to imply that the education system should simply be geared to producing people with practical skills who can immediately be put to work. Of course, this would be an enormous improvement on the present situation, since our country is desperate for creatively skilled manpower. However, there is more to education than this, as the writers of the 1960 KANU *Manifesto* realized. The system of education in a newly 'independent' nation like ours has the additional responsibility of producing self-confident, resourceful students. To serve the nation they must learn self-reliance and independence of thought and action. Since colonial penetration was not just material, but also psychological and spiritual, the primary role of education should have been to carry out intellectual and spiritual decolonization, and infuse our people with a new faith in their own capacities. But as we have seen, our rulers could not tolerate such a state of affairs, and so our schools continue to serve their old purpose: that of separating out an elite, which can then be superimposed on the people in order to prevent them discovering and using their own inner resources.

Perhaps some credit could be given to the education system we know if it produced competence in some sphere or other. But our graduates, through little fault of their own, are largely unable to make the leap from the theory or facts picked up in books or the lecture hall, to their application in life. They see themselves as superior to the manual labourer, and yet they cannot measure up to what is generally expected of the mental worker. They seem unable — or unwilling? — to make use of what they have learned. This is largely a problem of perception: in their eyes, the *status* that they attain because of their smattering of book-learning is enough. They seem to overlook the fact that is taken for granted in bourgeois capitalist societies: that status must be earned, and retained through merit, demonstrated competence, and productivity. Our educated stratum claim the status as a matter of right, without demonstrating the quality and responsibility which should go with it.

Thus, like their ruling mentors, they find themselves in lofty positions, and believe it their right to *supervise* the labour of others. They expect to be the managers and directors of enterprises, and the higher echelon bureaucrats. But since all their learning has taken place on the abstract level, they cannot really manage and lack the experience to direct. Their lack of practical experience and aversion to dirtying their hands means that their style of management is either irrelevant or ruinous. Whereas his Western equivalents would work their way up from the bottom, learning each stage of the work by direct experience, the Kenyan executive or manager simply expects to take over the position at or near the top by virtue of political influence or paper credentials. A sense of involvement and responsibility can only come from being immersed in a job — from knowing it thoroughly. It cannot simply come from a fancy title or hefty salary which allows the bearer to pose as the man in charge. For the most part, that sense is missing among those in leadership positions in Kenya. They generally, conspicuously lack dedication and, even more critically, accountability. They are always ready to dodge responsibility and blame. They are never taken to account for incompetence or even criminal wrong-doing; they are never fired outright. Instead, if they fail to manage one parastatal or ministry they are simply moved laterally to another high-paid chairmanship, or given medals. Thus, we have the curious situation in Kenya where mismanagement can frequently bring about promotion, and, as often as not, incompetence is rewarded.

Commitment as a Subversive Concept

But it would be wrong to imply that this incompetence, defective sense of responsibility and lack of dedication are general throughout the society. The truth is even more shameful. We do have individuals of talent and initiative who want nothing more than to dedicate their capabilities to their country, but they can find no way forward. The system penalizes excellence and integrity. By its very nature, it pulls down the few who seriously want to make a social contribution. Exceptional individuals who attempt to swim against the tide of mediocrity and *magendo* are targets of jealousy, suspicion, and intrigue. Bureaucrats and politicians cannot tolerate such energy and commitment. They feel personally threatened by those who do their work well — and refuse to grab on principle. Such people are considered quite mad. In our country, mediocrity brings its own rewards. Only those who play by the rules written by the men at the top will get ahead. Those who want to introduce demanding new standards will be thwarted at every step. Thus, the siphoning off of our material resources by foreign interests and their collaborators among the Kenyan bourgeoisie is matched by the squandering and destruction of our human resources. The handful of political leaders determined to serve the people and not merely their own interests find themselves detained, or out in the cold. Writers and religious leaders who insist on expressing the truth as they see it are considered renegades. Scientists with skills desperately needed by their country are unable to make headway in their fields, and are instead pushed into administration or petty business. Likewise, our tremendous raw talents in sports, music and theatre are almost completely overlooked (except when they go abroad) while second-rate foreign artists are nightly applauded in Nairobi.

It is not simply paranoia on the part of the ruling class which produces this aversion to excellence and competence. Instead, members of the ruling class fail to embrace or cultivate those aspects of bourgeois culture which even anti-bourgeois revolutionaries like Lenin believed necessary for the achievement of certain social and material goals. Indifferent to those bourgeois values that made European society so dynamic in the Nineteenth Century — to a

respect for thrift, hard work, and punctuality — our leaders operate
with a pre-capitalist mentality. They embrace the type of
conspicuous consumption which is the hallmark of a feudal ruling
caste, where the patron has to impress his dependent clients with
hollow pomp and lavish signs of his wealth and influence. They
respect the big belly squeezed under the steering wheel of the
Mercedes far more than they respect talent, quality, and
productivity. Perpetual parasites, they are simply not good enough
to be truly bourgeois.

Saidia Maskini

This endemic lack of respect for quality and achievement is one
manifestation of our failure as a people to achieve self-reliance and
self-rule. We appear a nation of beggars. What can be a more
eloquent commentary on this national 'dependency syndrome'
than the fact that with the exception of the occasional police
station or post office, our so-called 'independent' government
has never initiated and successfully carried through a single major
development project, without soliciting external assistance in
planning, finance, management and maintenance? When finally,
more likely than not with foreign prodding, government officials
decide upon a project, they demand the people's praise and
gratitude. As they see it, they are not simply doing their duty, but
bestowing favours. Meanwhile, instead of being put to productive
use, most public revenue has been consistently frittered away in
extravagant 'recurrent expenditure' by the managers of the theft-
economy.

After 20 years of 'independence' foreigners still train our army
and catch our criminals. They help run our ministries, our schools
and our hospitals. They plan our towns, roads, and even sewers.
They collect our taxes and influence our legal decisions. They write
our textbooks, own our newspapers, and even prepare our
development plans.

This state of continued dependence illustrates the failure of the
educational system in Kenya to instill self-confidence and faith
in our capacities as a people. Our rulers seem to find it more
natural to solicit foreign 'aid' than to harness the skills and energies
of Kenyans. They rely more and more on expatriate 'experts'. These
reputedly 'infallible' foreigners might actually have little in the way
of expertise and suitable experience, but that does not outweigh

their one great qualification: they are from the outside, and (in all likelihood) white. *Apana fikiri mzungu tarekebisha.* If anything goes wrong, outsiders will take care of it. This state of mind, developed during the colonial period, has yet to be shaken off. Our leaders — or many of them — remain pathetically eager to ape the white man in his absence, and to defer to him in his presence. As far as they are concerned, expensive imported 'experts' still have the answers. Even if these answers turn out to be totally mis-construed, or ill-suited to local conditions or simply not forth-coming, deference remains as a matter of habit. 'Experts' are never demoted or fired. They are encouraged to stay — both to keep an eye on things, and to provide employment for legions of *shamba* boys, houseboys, cooks, and maids.

As a result of this mendacity, of this excessive psychological and material dependence on external support and direction, our country has once again been carved into 'spheres of influence' dominated by foreign powers. Imperialist nations and their donor agencies now scramble to offer the latest programmes in 'development' and 'modernization' and the loans to finance them. Thus, Turkana is ceded to the USAID (USA), NORAD (Norway), the FAO (UN), and the EEC. Machakos is in the hands of the EEC which experiments in 'integrated rural development'. CIDA (Canada) meanwhile surveys and develops the rangelands, Belgium supplies water to Marsabit District, the World Bank plans and finances urban housing and waste disposal. Isiolo district is in a British sphere, while West Pokot is a Dutch one and Baringo a dual mandate of the World Bank and USAID's marginal lands project. York and Toronto Universities (Canada) oversee economic planning and train what they deem to be appropriate manpower. Multi-national companies control the commanding heights of our economy — they dominate industry, finance, agriculture, and trade — while the chief watch-dog of the system, the IMF, prepares to spring to the rescue should collapse threaten.

As often as not, these 'aid' agencies leave behind a trail of failed projects, like the 10 year USAID group ranching fiasco. They also leave behind outstanding loans, which must be repaid with interest. 'Aid' projects vary according to donor and locality, but in general it can be said that they are not self-sustaining. They make no attempt to teach self-reliance. Instead, they generally utilize pre-packaged imported techniques, which have little relevance to the 'sphere' upon which they are imposed. We can see this clearly in the case of the FAO irrigation project in Turkana. Once the

FAO pulls out, this expensive, unsuitable scheme, which at present produces less than 100 acres of crops for export will certainly fail. Some 'aid' projects, generally undertaken by church groups, are on a more modest scale, with some attempt being made to involve and train local participants. But most are simply 'given'. They are irrelevant 'gifts' from the outside world which, as often as not, awe or bewilder the recipients. Of course, the ruling bourgeoisie much prefers the large prestige projects, which allow enormous scope for pilfering. These 'showcase' projects are generally of a non-essential nature. For instance, the new Nairobi airport was a rich source of funds for the 'royal family'; as a functioning airport it has been little short of scandalous. The expensive pipeline project damaged the railway, which should have been used to transport oil. Kenya is meanwhile becoming criss-crossed with fancy tarmac roads going nowhere, which become footpaths for pedestrians and their livestock. Kiambu High School, built on an 'open plan' model when Kenya lacked teachers trained in such an approach and had no intention of training them in the future, absorbed money which could have built ten secondary schools, and has since reverted to an ordinary school at additional expense.

Only a naive observer would believe that projects such as these are intended to make our people self-reliant. Instead, they are part of the long-term political strategy of international capitalism. Their purpose is to extend political control, and to bend recipient economies to satisfy the needs of imperialist powers. Initially 'aid' donors were interested in long-term infrastructural projects like those involving roads, ports, and communications in order to facilitate the extraction of surpluses. Now the emphasis is on 'rural integrated development'. This tactic is designed to marginally improve the lives of rural populations and increase the production of primary commodities by peasants, in order to forestall explosive social unrest. The strategy aims to keep the people on the land, since the towns clearly will not be able to absorb them. The 'rural integrated development' approach at its most grandiose in Ukambani has mainly produced fat fees for expensive German consultants, while demoralized Kenyans do the spade work for a comparative pittance.

In the short run, some more suitable 'aid' projects — those which do not attempt to do too much, or which seek to meet a definite need, like the provision of piped water to rural settlements — do provide certain material gains. But those gains are meagre compared with the damage done in the long term. Kenya now has the dubious distinction of being one of the largest recipients of aid *in the world* and her dependence is growing at an alarming rate. If the American President has his way, in 1982 Kenya will get more than *twice* the 'aid' from the United States that it got in 1981.

Our future has been mortgaged by this continual reliance on outsiders to 'develop' our country for us. The practice of begging foreign help to prop up proven failures has, as in the case of Danish 'aid' to cereal parastatals, had the net effect of seriously undermining the economy. (See Appendix 7.) Not only are we chronically in debt to donor agencies, but also we are bogged-down mentally and spiritually. The habit of ingrained dependence leads us to mistrust our own capacities to rule ourselves. Our mental energy atrophies. We continue to expect salvation to come from the outside, instead of taking direct responsibility for our own lives and our own country.

Where Do We Go from Here?

As the situation now stands, our people are not encouraged to take that responsibility. Barred from meaningful participation in local and national life, they have turned inward, and once again seek out former solutions in order to deal with poverty, frustration and repression. We can detect disturbing signs of spiritual regression towards past forms. In both rural and urban areas there is a discernible return to superstition, as neighbour fears and resents neighbour and all struggle separately for survival under increasingly harsh conditions. Superstition is not only manifested by the rapidly proliferating Christian 'break-away' sects. Evidence also suggests that people are turning in greater numbers to the practice of witchcraft and magic as a way of coping with a largely hostile world and their isolation within it.

We must frankly come to terms with this deplorable state of affairs. While justly blaming the traitorous ruling class for betraying our aspirations, we must accept our own responsibility for allowing the situation to deteriorate to this extent, with little more sign of protest than occasional mutterings against the situation and haphazard individual resistance. Under the circumstances in which we find ourselves, it is crucial that we collectively rediscover our capacity to resist. For years we successfully conducted guerrilla warfare against the British: are we now too apathetic, uncaring or deluded to recognize that the active struggle for true independence must continue?

We must remember that everything of political value is a result of struggle. Those human rights which the citizens of 'independent' Kenya inherited and seem to take for granted — the vote, for instance, or the right to form trade unions — represent concrete gains of class struggle carried out by other people. We should not make the mistake of always expecting to be *given* what people elsewhere have *fought* to attain. Instead, we must determine once again to enter the fight ourselves, and struggle to regain and then extend political rights which our rulers would deny us, among them the right to associate and to express our interests collectively. In the process, we must seek ways to free ourselves from a perpetual dependency on others which has shackled the initiative of our people. Only by refusing to be passive and forever led — only through struggle — can we create a new reality and new mental outlook for ourselves, and in so doing enrich the totality of human experience.

5. Conclusion: *Twelekeeni*

We have demonstrated in the foregoing chapters that 'independence' is a hoax in Kenya. For independence to be more than a word, the colonized must take charge of their own affairs and obliterate colonial social and economic forms, creating fresh ones in all spheres. But in Kenya, the entire colonial system was passed on virtually intact, and has been perpetuated in a practically unchanged form over the last two decades. Instead of British governors and their P.C.s, we now have Kenyan governors and their P.C.s, using the same, or even more repressive, laws and institutions to subdue our people's expectations. Kenya's rulers have, in fact, surpassed the colonialists in their determination to eliminate popular participation and association and to ensure docility.

Political life in Kenya today parodies the promises made by KANU before 'independence'. The manoeuvring for personal influence, which today passes as 'politics', has been divorced from the activity of the broad masses of the people and left to a small clique surrounding a President who is himself above all criticism, acting more as a kind of sultan than an elected leader. The President and his select band control the State and use it to plunder the national wealth for their own personal profit and that of their international allies. But we must again emphasize that the enemy is not this or that individual or group of individuals. Those at the top are merely managers of a system which has trapped us into a dependency relationship with the capitalist West. Changes of personnel do not alter the essential character of that system, a system which is, of course, not unique to Kenya but is found throughout Africa and elsewhere. Kenya is by no means the only 'independent' country which has become a peripheral satellite of imperialist powers, West and East.

Therefore, the system is larger than any particular ruler, and it is

larger than Kenya. But having said as much, we cannot relieve our
so-called leaders from all responsibility for the predicament in
which we now find ourselves. Furthermore, we must face the
fact that our national condition will only get worse as ruling class
elements intensify their competition for the control of the State.
Their commitment to our future is nil. When things threaten to
fall apart they are ready to get on the first plane and go where
their money is. We are left behind to cope with the mess of their
making.

Due to their incompetence, greed and chronic mismanagement,
a period of prolonged chaos and economic and social disintegration
is, we fear, one likely future for Kenya. Such a future would be a
national catastrophe, destroying the few gains we have so far made
and further delaying the political development of our people. No
thinking person could anticipate such a future with relish.

What other possible futures might await us? We can foresee the
possibility of the following forms of change in the nature of the
regime. But given our present outlook and shaky structures, the
first three are considerably more likely than the others:

Coup d'etat
Coups, either military, or occasionally civilian, have become a way
of life in Africa. Some coups have been brought about by
imperialist intrigue. In most cases they involve the replacement
of one section of the ruling class by another section of the *same*
class. In most cases the public remains passive and does not
participate in the exchange of power. Coups rarely bring constructive change, but generally enrich the new clique and continue the
old system. For the most part coups occur when that old system
is endangered, and act to perpetuate it in a different guise. Thus, a
coup will become more and more likely as a way of preserving
the system as ruling class factionalism intensifies in Kenya. Such a
'solution' is merely temporary and never constructive. As the case
of Uganda demonstrates, all too often coups usher in the beginning
of the end — of a downward spiral into moral and social derange-
ment, culminating in national collapse.

Puppet State
Although most neo-colonies are client states of one or other
imperialist power, there can exist regimes which even more shame-
lessly hand over a measure of their sovereignty to a dominant
force, and merely exist on paltry 'rents' paid by such a power.

Zaire was moving in this direction when its government ceded vast tracts of the country to the West German company Otrag. It is possible that Kenya might come to this sort of an arrangement with the United States. The American 'strategic consensus' for the Indian Ocean—Persian Gulf—Southern Africa complex of interests has temporarily raised Kenya's strategic importance as a rearguard base for American and NATO 'Rapid Deployment Forces'. As the U.S. naval presence in the region grows, it is possible to foresee new deals being made, in which the Kenyan government will hand over more facilities and control to the superpower in exchange for loans and 'food aid'. An even more crippling state of dependency would be the result.

State Capitalism

There are numerous regimes, some nominally 'socialist', characterized by state ownership of large industrial, commercial and financial conglomerates or parastatals. Various 'isms' are invoked to cover up the extent to which these bodies, supposedly run for the benefit of 'the people', in fact operate in the interests of a small group of the population. Zambia's Christian 'Humanism' provides one such example. The large Zambian parastatals produce benefits for a handful of its people and not for the country, which remains perpetually poor in the midst of enormous natural wealth. In addition to disorganizing agricultural production, Kenya's parastatals and marketing boards seldom make any profit, and are mostly subsidized by taxation, but more parastatals could be created and State ownership extended if the few could thereby ensure their own well-being. This system shares with the others we have discussed a basic disregard for mass participation in economic or political decision-making.

Other less likely directions in which our country may move include the following:

Bourgeois Capitalism

With due respect to the argument that capitalism has rarely conformed to a 'classical' pattern of development, and that it might yet stimulate industrial 'take-off' in neo-colonies like Kenya, we must state that we see little sign of that happening. In Kenya, the infrastructure is geared to meet the needs of outside interests. Productivity is low and falling. There is little indication that the country will develop its own capital goods industry, a vital component of industrial 'take-off'. Instead, self-sustaining economic growth seems certainly as far away now as it was at 'independence'. We thus have in Kenya an inefficient, deformed economy, with a small domestic market and weak regional trade links. The Kenyan economy is essentially unproductive: a kind of drain for the out-flow of surplusses. Profits accumulate outside the country, in the hands of the international capitalists and members of the contemptible 'indigenous bourgeoisie' who bank abroad. The latter bear little resemblance to the inventive, dynamic entrepreneurs whose risk-taking and ruthless sense of efficiency and thrift fuelled industrial 'take-off' in Nineteenth Century Europe and America.

Populism
Here we must make a distinction between a half-hearted harnessing of what can be termed 'populist solutions' to damp down social discontent, and a thoroughly democratic populist system. Under the former, a government seeks to appease the population by carrying out minor reforms — especially in land ownership, or some aspects of foreign control of the economy — or by vociferously embracing cultural nationalism. At first, this approach may seem progressive, because it might lead to more of the wealth being spread more widely in the society. But this approach has serious weaknesses, depending as it does on the 'good heart' of a benevolent ruler who blocks organized participation by the people in their own affairs. It is a fragile system which lasts as long as the 'good man' lasts. There is evidence that imperialist powers or internal reactionaries can easily undermine such a regime, if it is in their interests to do so.

   As opposed to pseudo-populism, genuine populism is a democratic and egalitarian system in which authority flows from the people up to their leaders. Such a system, possessing close affinities with socialism, demands that the people be in control of their resources and how they are used. This sort of populism is highly unlikely in Kenya.

African Socialism
Many African regimes have sought to disguise class antagonisms and inequalities by declaring themselves to be 'African Socialist'. They then go on to glorify a mythical African past where, in theory, all people were nice to each other and all shared communally the wealth produced communally. The proponents of this view state

that class struggle is biologically and culturally alien to Africans, and is part of a 'foreign ideology'. In practice, African Socialism generally protects and nourishes a neo-colonial dependency with imperialist-oriented economies. Kenya's Sessional Paper No. 10 on African Socialism (1965) is an excellent example of this kind of deception. Tanzania's *Ujamaa* is currently still masquerading as an experiment in 'socialism', while the country slips deeper and deeper into dependency and bankruptcy. Such African Socialist regimes generally depend on the outside world, even for basics such as food. Foreigners and ruling cliques carry on accumulating, while preaching the virtues of 'shared poverty'. The people remain largely passive, and democratic organizations are not tolerated. In short, the word 'socialism' — detached from its social and economic moorings — is merely bandied about by these regimes to cover their innate inadequacies with a cloak of morality.

Scientific Socialism
Unlike the 'African' parody, scientific socialism cannot be reduced to a set of bureaucratic declarations imposed on the people. It cannot simply be 'decreed'. Rather, this most progressive of social systems must emerge from a long revolutionary process and fierce class struggle, culminating in the overthrow of the entire capitalist system of production and social relations. As the histories of the USSR and China demonstrate, during the transition to socialism intense class struggle continues, and there is a constant danger of regression to brutal statist domination. That danger is lessened if certain preconditions for the attainment of socialism have already been realized by the society at large. These preconditions include a high level of economic productivity, and a politically-conscious people led by a politically-uncompromising party which is prepared to wage revolutionary civil war to uproot the old order when the people are ready for it. Neither of these preconditions is present in Kenya today.

We recognize that years of deprivation of basic rights of expression and association have de-politicized our people, and eroded the gains which we had made during the armed struggle against colonialism. Neither are we yet in the position to demand an end to the plundering of our economy by foreigners, and the reduction of over-consumption by our indigenous bourgeoisie — demands which must be achieved before we can hope to raise our general level of productivity. With our background, and in our present circumstances, it seems idle to talk of a true socialist alternative to the current regime. Socialism will not descend to us like manna from heaven.

Instead of indulging in wishful thinking we can — and must — get our sense of direction, and determine what must be done to bring about a situation in which socialism *can* be considered a realistic alternative for Kenya. The first step is an obvious one: we Kenyans must learn that we, and we alone, must take responsibility for our national future. We must refuse to remain passive recipients of what is given from above, and instead, fully participate to initiate and direct change. That is the immediate task. It is over-whelmingly political. We must at once seek to revive principled discussion on *issues* in order to prepare the way for self-assertion and active involvement of the people. We must find ways to articulate and defend our interests, independent of bosses or patrons, forming our own institutions in the process based on popular mass participation. We must realize that *anything* that lessens dependency in practical terms or opposes dependency, even symbolically, represents a move in the right direction, and is part of our re-education as a people.

Thus, we must accumulate a stock of practical acts, large and small, and symbolic gestures which can be used to raise the level of political awareness about the nature of our predicament. These acts and gestures involve defiance. We must be determined to pay the price of defying the machinery of coercion which keeps us dispersed, disunited, and repressed. We must hold meetings in defiance of invidious permit regulations, and discuss all ways of capturing the initiative before the situation becomes even more critical. We must gather together in small groups of perhaps three or four, to speak and listen to each other — not simply to gain knowledge and understanding, but to plan how best to *act*. Our point of unity is principled opposition to a destructive neo-colonial system. Unity born of this opposition overshadows those differences which may divide us at other levels. In the process of coming together, we must learn to cast off our meekness and feelings of deference for authority, recognizing that our so-called leaders are not worthy of our reverence and respect. Instead, we must learn to respect *each other*, and to work in co-operation. We must support each other, and look to ourselves, not to our 'leaders' to find the way forward. The future of our nation and our children depends on our willingness to take risks and to act to alter the situation. Once we embark on the path of defiance, we will discover that one little spark can set a fire alight. The spirit of principled unity will weld our people into small groups, small groups in larger groups, and finally the nation will become fully mobilized.

Obviously, the current regime is too weak and insecure to allow such developments to take place openly. It will seek a brutal repression of all democratic forms. We must not be quelled, but instead learn from the examples of other peoples who have fought their way out of similar situations, as well as from our own past experiences. In the past we have practiced mass defiance: we can do so again.

It is encouraging to see numerous signs of rebellion against authority in our country today. For instance, popular underground literature is spreading, despite rigid state controls, and people's songs more and more express resistance. Workers, disgusted by union collusion with the government, have organized themselves in defiance of anti-strike laws, and there are attempts to form genuine trade unions which foster the workers' interests. Farmers have rebelled against exploitation by burning sugar cane in Nyanza, uprooting cash-crops, boycotting marketing boards, and even fighting corrupt co-operatives and police in Central Province. The next obvious stage is for them to seize idle land and cultivate it for our people's food needs. The largely spontaneous nation-wide school and University 'riots' constitute a strong indication of things to come.

Thus far, acts of defiance are isolated and uncoordinated. We must learn from our past mistakes, and find ways to organize and direct them. In the past, political militancy in Kenya was largely elitist. The masses were seldom involved in the initial organizational stages, and afterwards there was little attempt to create a political infrastructure among the population. Furthermore, political movements in Kenya suffered from a lack of ideological clarity, and the tendency to fall back on 'tribalism' as a political base in the absence of a larger ideological commitment. Perhaps these organizational and ideological weaknesses were all that could be expected at that stage of national development. We must, however, move beyond that stage now, and build on the past instead of repeating it.

Our orientation and re-education must recognize the realities of class formation in Kenya. As recent studies of class in Kenya make clear, although class formation may not be following the 'classic' European pattern, there are certainly groups exploiting others in our society, and appropriating for themselves the surplus which others create. It only delays our political emancipation to seek tribal, regional, or racial explanations of what are in fact *class* divisions. Ultimately, we must be able to think beyond the boundaries of artificially-created nation-states like Kenya, and be aware that class struggle has an international dimension. That international dimension can only gain in importance in the future, as the growing power of the multinational corporations increasingly renders nation-states subordinate, and even obsolete. The struggle to make this or that country socialist must finally merge in the larger struggle to defeat capitalism globally.

But for the present, however, we must work realistically within the framework of the nation-state. We must now undertake the initial steps of defiance which can act as a trigger for the disciplined mobilization of our people. It is not for us to formulate a clear-cut recipe for that mobilization and resulting social change. Such change is not a simple matter of prescription, but emerges from the concrete strategies and alliances formed during struggle. In the process of struggle our people will learn to create their own vigorous forms of expression, to revitalize their own culture, and to find a cure for mental apathy and the destructive habits of dependency. What better legacy can we leave future Kenyans?

Appendices: A Sampling of How the System Works

Appendix 1

KANU: The Second 'Dynamic' Decade

KANU is an illegal organization. The Registrar requires that to remain legal, any organization must hold annual meetings and present annual returns: neither requirement has been met by KANU. Even on its own terms, it lacks constitutional legality. The party constitution stipulates that party elections be held every two years, and that there be annual meetings of the national executive and branch delegations. There were, however, *no* elections at the national level between 1966 and 1978. After the murder of the KANU General Secretary Tom Mboya in 1969, Robert Matano was the 'Acting' General Secretary until he was confirmed in office by the October 1978 elections. These elections, so long overdue, were only held in 1978 because of the necessity of giving some kind of legality to Kenyatta's successor.

At present the party appears to be operating without any constitution whatever. In order to get rid of the anti-Odinga device of having eight vice-presidents (created by the Limuru Conference of 1966) and in order to include new provisions barring former KPU detainees from contesting elections, an amended constitution was drawn up in 1974 but was never presented to the delegates conference for ratification. As the 1966 constitution is, therefore, technically valid, KANU is seven vice-presidents short.

The existence of this illegal organization is perpetuated in order to determine who should be given access to political office. KANU is thus a 'party' without politics. The only 'issue' which interests most of those who scramble for office is, will they or won't they get close enough to the centre of power to feed themselves and their connections at the nation's expense. During the jostling for position, two broad factional groups emerged in the 1970's: a pro-Moi, anti-GEMA group, and a pro-GEMA, anti-Moi group. At stake was the succession, and the spectacular looting which went along with the job at the top.

From time to time KANU 'revitalization' drives would be called by one or the other faction in order to further their fortunes. A 'revitalization' drive had been announced in 1970, as a way of diverting attention from the murder of Mboya, another one was proclaimed in 1975 in order to counter criticism of the government cover-up of J.M. Kariuki's murder, and a third membership drive was due to take place in late 1978 to provide the new President with a power base. All of these 'revitalization' attempts came to nothing. In October 1975, the Deputy Speaker of the House and another M.P. were detained for conceding that KANU was dead. Five years later, the party General Secretary practically admitted as much, saying that KANU had performed poorly as a political party and only showed signs of life during election time.

'Life' usually boiled down to racketeer style arm-twisting during blatantly corrupt 'membership drives'. Membership to KANU was supposedly granted on payment of shs. 2 a year. In spite of this token payment, there were probably only about one million members in the 1970's — the General Secretary had no idea of the proper membership figures. The announcement that grass-roots elections were about to be held brought out the politicians to recruit their 'own' members. Politicians would buy up membership books from P.C.s in order to keep them out of the hands of opponents. They would then distribute tickets to their own supporters. It is not surprising that such 'recruitment drives' produced many cases of forged membership tickets, and more 'voters' at local and branch levels than registered members. As for the funds collected by party officials during 'recruitment drives' — such money never found its way to party coffers, and the party never issued public statements about its accounts.

Neither did it stick to its own election timetables. The Acting General Secretary Matano proved himself an obedient stooge of whatever faction had the upper hand at the moment, and a master of the art of double-speak and about-turn. Highlights of his (and the party's) performance in the 1970s include the following:

1972-3: national executive elections repeatedly announced and then postponed, with Matano listing such reasons for the cancellations as the interference of the OAU All-Africa Trade Fair, the failure to publish the amended party constitution, and the proximity of the general elections. The real reason behind dithering on elections was the intensification of political in-fighting between the GEMA group and its rivals.

1974–6: grass-roots elections and factional membership drives, as the 'Change-the-Constitution' group tried to block Moi's succession.

Late 1976: Matano announced that branch elections would be held by the end of the year. These were subsequently postponed until 7 February 1977. Meanwhile, the party issued several contradictory directives about membership drives, and quarrels over stolen membership receipt books and forged tickets made the party seem better off 'dead'.

3 March 1977: Matano announced that national elections for KANU would take place within the month. The date was finally set for 3 April 1977. Delegates had gathered in Nairobi for voting, when elections were indefinitely postponed. Matano made the announcement on April Fool's Day, and attributed it to 'circumstances beyond our control': circumstances which included the sudden illness of Mzee, and the GEMA group's fear that they would not be able to strong-arm their candidates into leading party positions.

4 October 1978: following the death of Mzee, national executive elections were finally held to confirm Moi as President. Once these were out of the way, attention was focussed on forthcoming general elections which demonstrated the depth of voter apathy. The drive to register voters in mid-1979 was a dismal exercise, with most districts not even reaching their 1974 levels. Kenyans clearly viewed 'their' party with something less than enthusiasm. 'Democratic' decision-making was now given some new twists, with continual disputes over who was a party member and who was not, over stolen membership books, and over the sale of membership receipts for personal gain. Matano announced that all candidates for elections at all levels, parliamentary and civic, had to be life members of KANU, which meant they had to pay shs. 1000. He also announced all had to be 'cleared' by the party before contesting seats, a swipe at the former KPU detainees and other politicians whose presence in parliament could conceivably prove an embarrassment. In August 1979, the issue of 'life membership' appeared anything but a straightforward one. Matano claimed that anyone who purchased life membership from anywhere but party headquarters would have to pay again, since those endorsed elsewhere could be forged or 'signed in a funny way'.

Other party officials opposed Matano's orders. Among those barred because of their 'funny' life membership receipts were Odinga and other ex-KPU members. In some cases, life membership money was not accepted for undisclosed 'special reasons'. The whole election exercise boiled down to a cynical manipulation of 'democratic' forms, and an unabashed attempt to cook the results by using party machinery to do the government's dirty work.

There is little sign that the party is becoming more respectable in the 1980s. Instead, it continues to be held in low esteem, its members bullied, and its officials trotted out now and again to axe political undesirables. Members of the KANU Parliamentary Group are instructed how to vote and threatened if they do not toe the government's line. M.P.s now vote with their feet — the habitual lack of a quorum in the House represents a form of protest. In February 1981 grass-roots elections were postponed so that 'people can plant their crops'; they were tentatively planned for April and then postponed indefinitely.

Meanwhile, Matano continues to issue his funny announcements. In June 1980 he sent out a radio message ordering party branch chairmen and secretaries to attend a workshop in Nairobi *on the following day* because, in his words, the party was not functioning satisfactorily, and because the West Germans had paid for such a workshop and wanted to observe it. Delegates assembled in an angry and confused mood to find that there was no agenda for the workshop. They were then treated to the spectacle of the inner circle 'eating' German money. This abysmal lack of sense of direction and prevailing interest of party officials with lining their own pockets, typify the party's role in national life.

In April 1981, party officials again bowed to instructions from the President and banned Odinga from standing for the Bondo parliamentary seat. A hatchet job was then organized through the courts to get a despicable stooge nominated unopposed for the seat. Odinga had been accused of maligning the dead by claiming that Kenyatta had grabbed land. Clearly the last thing that the ruling clique wishes to hear is anything resembling the truth. The 'wise' decision to ban Odinga and use the courts to do government dirty work was loudly applauded by branch chairmen anxious to prove their dedication to 'peace, love and unity' and loyalty to the big boss.

In Busia South, similar machinations ensured the appointment of an old trusty from KADU days. However, after the decision on

Busia, our stalwart General Secretary found himself being clobbered with a *rungu* by his treasurer who claimed he did not like one of Matano's candidates. At about the same time the party President announced at Kericho that M.P.s will be under the supervision of the chief *mnyapara* (himself) in their constituency affairs, since they were merely KANU foremen. The President would henceforth interfere to 'rescue voters' from their M.P.s if necessary: 'decisions reached by KANU are final and no one has the mandate to challenge them.' Shortly after, the nation was treated to the first sycophantic call that Moi should be big boss for life, since 'the *nyayo* philosophy had made the country achieve a lot.' At this rate the third decade of KANU's tenuous existence is likely to prove even less inspiring — and more destructive — than the previous two.

Appendix 2

The City Hall Smorgasbord

Among the top looters must be numbered the Nairobi city councillors and other city officials. Our nation's wealth is concentrated in the capital, and the members of the Nairobi City Council are not about to miss the opportunities for personal enrichment which the city affords. Only a fool among them would hang back when the goodies are within such easy reach, and are so profuse.

And so the wise city fathers are into everything that's going. Perhaps their biggest meals are in the tendering business. They are fond of bribes and have their own clients whom they would push forward. Sometimes the promotion of particular favourites can get a bit embarrassing, as in the case of the World Bank funded Chania-Thika water project which involved interference from all quarters, and has left the World Bank with a big headache and the City Council with large legal liabilities. Under these circumstances, tenders end up meaning nothing. The lucky clients who bag the jobs inevitably push up prices because of the necessity of covering the cost of bribes. Projects undertaken by the City Council seldom reach completion. More generally, they are suspended because of escalating costs, or — as in the case of the city's sewerage works — because the contractor absconded with the funds.

Another lucrative area which has stimulated the appetites of councillors and other city officials is the housing business. The

Minister for Local Government — an ex-mayor himself — recently baffled the City Council by announcing a new one man/one house policy. Fortunately for our hefty eaters, no one (least of all the Minister) took it seriously. Most councillors have several plots in the 'low cost' Umoja housing project. A favourite tactic is to take plots out in the name of wives (the more the better) and children. The sponsor of the project, USAID, got so perturbed by City Council fraudulence that it threatened to pull out altogether. But the city fathers don't feel a bit ashamed. After all, *their* housing — that which had been designed for councillors in the middle of City Park — has been grabbed by ministers and top businessmen, forcing the councillors to move on to whatever is going. They have begun to sub-divide the suburb of Karen, despite the lack of sufficient water, and are particularly attracted to public playgrounds and open space which they feel no qualms about taking over for their personal use. Another device to keep hunger at bay is the sub-letting of City Council houses, at up to ten times the market price. Since many city officials have taken additional houses in the names of relatives, sub-letting can yield up a tidy income.

Some city employees, especially those with their own drug companies, prefer to do their fiddling in the medical department. Drug companies with City Council connections do a roaring trade. Things have a way of disappearing from City Council medical stores and clinics. City officials steal medical supplies which they can sell off elsewhere, leaving clinics to dole out injections of aspirin and water. They also have access to City Council vehicles, spare parts and other Council supplies. They rake in kick-backs, they embezzle money, and they act as Mafia-style bosses in slum neighbourhoods where they are landlords and control kiosks and markets. No activity is too lowly to escape their attention.

What is taking place in Nairobi is therefore a kind of concentrated version of what is happening in the nation at large. In Nairobi, as in the nation, there is only one issue in 'politics'; who will have access to office and its spoils? Nairobi City politics have likewise revolved around rivalry between the GEMA-backed Family and a shifting, motley group of opponents. City Council politics in the early 1970's saw Matano in action in an old role but new guise — as Minister for Local Government he had to carry out the job in which he, as Acting General Secretary of KANU, had so much practice; that of postponing elections. Mayoral elections were postponed time and time again because the incumbent mayor (the President's daughter) feared she would not be re-elected. After she finally bowed out, the same old factional squabbles continued, since the Family group was loathe to hand over sole looting rights to their victorious opponents. In an attempt to embarrass the new mayor in 1977, the GEMA die-hards went so far as to organize a probe into Council wrongdoing. During their days of 'eating' no such probe had been contemplated. Clearly they were simply out to discredit the Council so that it would be disbanded by the government, like councils in Mombasa, Kisumu and Kiambu. The Town Clerk ordered councillors not to co-operate with the probe, and the whole thing was allowed to fizzle out when its originators feared that some of their own misdeeds might come to light if it continued.

So much for the first attempt to 'clean up' City Hall. The second attempt was equally farcical. In late 1979, a new 'populist' mayor was installed: his 'populism' was a similar brand to the President's. Both President and mayor were out to fool the public into believing that they would make relentless war on corruption and initiate a new era of wholesome government. In fact, they were simply out to clear the decks for their own bout of grabbing, and disguise their true intentions. The 'clean up' initiated by the new mayor was designed to cover up the mistakes of *nyayo* men and expose the crimes committed by their opponents. The probe, begun in February 1980, got a little further than its predecessor. The C.I.D. finally charged four councillors with assault and theft. These four were selected because of their position in factional politics, not because they were more violent or crooked than their colleagues. There were in addition two large sacrificial goats left over from the previous regime: the Town Clerk and the head of the medical department. Someone had to appear to take the blame for the numerous health and housing scandals, in order for the public to be appeased and the looting to go on unabated. No criminal charges were brought against these men, despite the disappearance of millions of shillings during their tenure in office.* The loss of their jobs was deemed substantial enough punishment, and so they were sent, over their strong objections, on 'compulsory leave', no doubt with full retirement benefits. That was the end of the new regime's 'clean up' campaign.

As the 'populist' mayor and Council carry on in typical City Hall

---

* in all cases where specific figures are quoted in these Appendixes, these are publicly-reported *auditable* figures which would fall far short of the actual sums in question.

style, the city itself slips further and further into chaos. Administering is not the administration's strong point. The Council seems remarkably insensitive to the needs of the city's inhabitants. Their idea of how to carry out a housing policy is to send the *askaris* to bulldoze shanties.

They can demolish, but not build. No wonder that residents of poorer neighbourhoods see little difference between the present Council and its colonial predecessor. Neither does the Council shine in matters of education. Its more than 100 primary schools are over-crowded and under-supplied, while 50,000 children in the city are without school places. So disastrous is Council health administration that the city has suffered several cholera epidemics and two bouts of plague since 1979. Malaria has made a triumphant return to town, and dysentry is endemic. To complete this hygienic picture, in the City Mortuary bodies can lie rotting for up to three years.

Meanwhile the fabric of the city deteriorates on a class basis. In the wealthy suburbs, there is an attempt to maintain the streets and street lighting. Rubbish is regularly collected from outside locked gates; inside the gates, cars are frequently washed and lawns watered. On the other side of town, in the eastlands, it is a different story. Here, residents often go without drinking water, and live their lives amid uncollected garbage. The Council once again maintains its colonial traditions.

It will take more than a cover-up 'probe' or two to change the ways of the City Council. The way things are going, our capital city does not have much of a future. The Council is chronically in debt, although it would like to ignore this fact by refusing to keep records and accounts. During the last few years, it has been diverting hundreds of millions of shillings from their intended use in order to keep things limping along. It constantly budgets for deficits, and relies on the World Bank to bail it out of trouble. Recently, it underlined its grave financial position by ordering property rates to be raised by up to 1000%. The subsequent public outcry has forced the Council to withdraw its new rates sheet. Nairobi residents might well wonder what 'services' their councillors will provide them with next. Judging from recent council history, they should be prepared for the worst.

Appendix 3

Living with Multinationals: Rivatex and Firestone

The large multinational corporations are transnational, and have no fixed abode. They are beyond the control of the nation-state and are beginning to bring its future existence into doubt. Weak, artificial states have little leeway in bargaining with multinationals, which can with ease shift their spheres of operations if their 'hosts' seem less than totally accommodating. Kenya has generally seemed a most co-operative host, on the surface at least. As the following case studies demonstrate, the Kenyan government has invited in multinationals on extremely favourable terms, and put their well-being above that of the local capitalists and consumers. However, the subsequent relationship between the government and the multinational has not always progressed smoothly, since well-placed individuals within government and business circles have often, in breach of the government's contract with the multinationals, insisted on getting a share of the action. Their looting activities and smuggling of goods can, as in the Firestone example, sabotage monopoly agreements reached by corporation and government. In the case of Rivatex, foreign directors have insisted that the government enact and enforce stringent controls over the textile industry as the price of its continuing operations. But whether multinationals pull out or stay, they are unlikely to be damaged in any major way by the undermining of their monopoly control over the market. Their economies are too resilient for that. The same cannot be said of the Kenyan economy. Kenyan taxpayers initially pay a heavy price to subsidize the presence of multi-nationals, and are left to pick up the bills and survey the wreckage when they leave.

Rivatex
Rivatex was incorporated in 1975 after the multinational textile company Seditex was selected to be a partner with the government in textile manufacture. Rivatex was formed as a private company based in Eldoret, with Seditex supplying the greater part of equity capital, the management, and technical expertise. The company immediately assumed the position of near monopoly. It was exempt from sales tax and import duties; it did not have to declare its dividends, and no controls were exercised over its repatriation of profits. It could appoint its own distributors and because of the

101

composition of its Board of Directors it helped design government policy for the entire textile market.

There is little that is 'Kenyan' about Rivatex. When it started production in 1977 it had approximately 1,500 shareholders — these included two Swiss finance groups, an American corporation, and two German trading companies. Less than half the total shares were owned by ICDC, which is itself largely funded by foreign loans and the West German government. The company was, therefore, almost totally dominated by foreign capital. Directors included several businessmen of German, French, Swiss, and Israeli extraction. The Kenyans on the Board were acting in a purely comprador capacity, having vital links with the Ministry of Commerce as well as several other key directorships. Real control was exercised by the Seroussi brothers based in Hamburg, Germany, who direct the action from afar through their comprador agents. It was pressure by the Seroussi brothers which led the government to crack down on textile smuggling, and restrict and then ban altogether imports of second-hand clothing. The facade of monopoly thus exists, although of course prominent individuals and their wives continue to bring in fashion garments through normal channels and the V.I.P. lounge. The Kenyan consumer is the loser, being forced to buy over-priced shoddy goods and being deprived of imported second-hand clothing which was all most working Kenyans could afford. Recently, it was announced that individuals will no longer be allowed to bring foreign clothes into Kenya, not even for charity. Personal clothing can now be seized at the discretion of customs officials. Meanwhile local capitalists in the textile industry have been consistently undermined and are very bitter at the government protection afforded a multinational. The company's one potential competitor — the Nanyuki Textile Mill (jointly owned by Lonrho and the German Development Bank) opened in 1976 and went into liquidation in 1977, leaving the field to Rivatex. Symbolic of its privileged position, Rivatex even has a monopoly in its designs of the 'protected word' *nyayo*!

Firestone

Government-multinational co-operation has not been so smooth in the case of Firestone. In 1969 the government chose the Firestone Tyre Company over two competitors for a ten year monopoly of the Kenyan tyre market. Its leading competitor, Dunlop, had tendered a proposal offering a less capital-intensive project employing twice as many people and using second-hand machinery. Despite the fact that lower-priced tyres would have been produced by Dunlop, the government chose Firestone because it promised a higher initial capital investment and was willing to use only African distributors (most of whom later failed in business). Firestone had the ear of two key ministers who insisted it get the contract.

The contract was a very advantageous one for the company: the government promised to ban rival imports; Firestone was allowed to import duty-free all its machinery and materials; it had absolute managerial control (it was happy to include prominent ministerial relatives on the Board) and it could fix its own prices and high technical fees. The Company then demonstrated its strength by forcing the Nairobi City Council to rearrange an already built transnational highway in accordance with its wishes and against those of the Planning Committee.

But things were more shaky in the tyre market. Firestone apparently began by bringing in second-hand equipment from Zambia, which was a clear violation of the contract. The original agreement had provided for heavy protection from outside competition, but the establishment of the General Tyre Company in Tanzania, and Family smuggling of Michelin tyres from 1973 on, flooded the Kenyan market and forced the factory to operate at under-capacity. This meant that tyre prices had to be pushed up further.

Having been unable to use its plant at full capacity early in the 1970s, the company was incapable of producing to meet demand later in the decade. The closure of the border with Tanzania, smuggling of Firestone tyres from Kenya to neighbouring Sudan and Uganda, the large increase in numbers of cars following in the wake of the coffee boom, and the enlarged demand for tyres by the vehicle assembly plants, all resulted in a severe tyre shortage by 1978. In 1978 the company was only capable of producing 270,000 units a year, when 360,000 were needed. The quality of its products was causing great concern, and innumerable deaths on the highways. But the company also had its grievances. In its view government had consistently failed to live up to its side of the contract with Firestone, neglecting to protect the company from foreign imports (which meant lucrative pickings for ministers and their friends) and backing down on its pricing agreements.

At the end of the 1970s, the government conducted a feasibility study towards setting up a second tyre company. However, no foreign company was interested since the government had the reputation of failing to live up to its agreements. Furthermore, Firestone itself has shown no inclination to expand. Instead, it is running its factory at top capacity day and night, and is running down its machinery. When the machinery is completely worn out it is likely that Firestone will shut down its plant and leave the country. It will take with it hefty profits, and leave behind a few Kenyans enriched by a decade's tyre racketeering. Once again, we will lose.

Appendix 4

The Fertilizer Fiasco

A recent editorial in a national newspaper reported that a new firm, National Agricultural Chemicals and Fertilisers Ltd., had been set up with the advice of 'consultants of international repute' to provide the country with fertilizers. The editorial claimed that one of the 'greatest blows' to Kenya's farmers had been the 'ignominious failure' of the shs. 400 million government-sponsored Ken-Ren fertilizer manufacturing company at the hands of 'international confidence tricksters'. The chairman of the new firm assured the nation that now the fertilizer industry would forge ahead and 'avoid the fruitless and expensive efforts of the past'.

The official line for the abortive attempt to set up a fertilizer company in Mombasa in 1975-78 thus places the blame squarely with international capital, and the swindlers who victimized the Kenyan government and our nation's farmers and left behind a pile of useless, rusting equipment when they absconded with the funds. The true story of the Ken-Ren failure is a good deal more complex and damning of the government. Ken-Ren Chemicals and Fertilizers Ltd had been created in 1975 as a joint venture of the government and N-Ren, an American agro-chemical firm, with a formal contract signed in April 1975. Initially, the project was delayed by the problem of securing a site at Mombasa. The government had promised a harbour site, but after one and a half years of doing nothing finally offered an unsuitable hilltop site which would cost more than 40 times more to prepare for use. This was only the beginning of the company's trouble. The Family had meanwhile recognized the millions to be made from fertilizer imports, and set out to sabotage the project. The Ministry of

Agriculture in 1977 granted certain well-placed businessmen
contracts for huge fertilizer imports, in violation of its agreement
with Ken-Ren. About the same time a group of powerful Kenyans
purchased the Windmill Fertiliser Company to import fertilizer
from abroad. Clearly a successfully functioning company would
conflict with these interests.

And so the company had to be killed. The agent of destruction
was a new 'executive chairman' of the company, whose position
was created by the government in contradiction with the agreement
with the company. Appropriately enough, the man appointed as
'executive chairman' was the man who later became managing
director of the fertilizer firm to be set up on the ruins of Ken-Ren.
Without going into too many details, we can say that he did his
job well, coming into immediate conflict with the existing expatriate
managing director who was promptly deported. After that, the
executive chairman had a relatively easy time slowing down
operations and finally bringing the company into liquidation. At
first he insisted that a new feasibility study be carried out: its
report was submitted after a further delay of a year and a half,
and showed everything to be in order. Not to be deterred, the
executive chairman, at the prompting of the powerful interests
he represented, then insisted that the management contract with
Ken-Ren be renegotiated, which would cause further insupportable
delays and certainly jeopardize the entire project. While government
renegotiations dragged on, the executive chairman sabotaged
operations in more concrete ways. Expensive equipment was
allowed to rust at the Mombasa dock because the chairman refused
to clear it through Customs. Finally the government decided to
give the company its *coup de grace*, and in June 1978 the plant
site was taken away from Ken-Ren. Since more than $8 million
had been spent by the company clearing the site, it was now
valuable industrial land and of use to 'someone'. After this, the
company was forced into liquidation, with shs. 400 million going
down the drain and our farmers finding themselves starved of
fertilizer at a time of world-wide shortage.

After heaping the blame on 'international confidence tricksters'
when in fact it rests squarely with a clique of Kenyan looters, the
government appeared to let the matter rest. There was no official
inquiry into the loss of hundreds of millions of shillings. Then, in
January 1979, the President announced that a new fertilizer plant
was being contemplated for Mombasa. By this time the Ken-Ren
project could have been in operation. Nothing was done for the

next two years. In February 1981, there were reports that Kenya's fertilizer supplies were almost exhausted, and that the government had to beg for stocks from Norway, Japan, and America. Then came the news that it had signed an agreement with a Dutch company for a fertilizer factory to be built on the old Ken-Ren site at Mombasa. Surprisingly, since this announcement a subsequent Sessional Paper on food policy fails to mention the construction of such a plant. However, even if the project does go forward, it will not be operational until 1982 at least, by which time costs would have greatly escalated, and farm production suffered more reverses. To quote our editorial again: 'Farmers need this commodity urgently. It must be made a top priority project. Regular progress reports should be published to reassure the farmers that the undertaking is not another Ken-Ren.' A final word to the profit-seeking Dutch: beware!

Appendix 5

Land Racketeering

Land policy in 'independent' Kenya has faithfully perpetuated the colonial land tenure system. The catch phrase 'willing seller willing buyer' rationalizes the concentration of property in the hands of a few politically-powerful individuals, and the growing landlessness of the poor. There are few other transactions which have been as uniformly scandalous as those involving private and public land. Below are some examples, organized in two sections — the first concerns the transfer of public land to influential individuals, while the second deals with the exploitation of the landless by bogus 'land buying' companies.

In the mid-1970s, Parliament attempted on two separate occasions to set up select committees to enquire into corruption. These committees were to have broad terms of reference, but their main concern was the excessive acquisition of farm-land, of national parkland, and of urban property by members of the inner ruling circle and their associates. The committees were dismantled before they could even start work. Later, in October 1978, it was reported in a compilation by the Commissioner of Lands, that the majority of public land transactions in Nairobi involved the same handful of politically-influential individuals. Among the deals cited was the

excision of precious railways land, which was then transferred to a
non-existent company at a loss to the public of more than shs. 30
million. About the same time, one individual obtained an estimated
200 acres of premium industrial real-estate in Nairobi. The scramble
for public land did not end there. Individuals — including
councillors and government officials — got their hands on such
public utility land as school reserves (e.g. Kenya High School),
residential playgrounds, and the like. A typical example is the
carving up of City Park, ostensibly for housing for councillors.
By 1980, after the President had given substantial gifts of land to
three key political supporters, there was no government land left
in Nairobi.

Land scandals have not been confined to Nairobi. In 1978 it was
reported that top politicians and civil servants in Nakuru were
using government funds to purchase private plots, farms, and to
finance private houses. According to the Permanent Secretary in
the Office of the President, an estimated shs. 100 million was
diverted to these ends. Typically, police investigations into this
high-level theft were called off after a few minor characters had
been convicted on trumped-up charges. In Mombasa, a P.C. was
given primary school land, and there has been a continuing free-for-
all among prominent politicians and civil servants for valuable beach
property. Elsewhere in urban areas the story is a similar one, as
premium public land has been put up for grabs.

At the other end of the scale from the land sharks are the
landless. In theory at least land-buying companies did offer poor
people a unique opportunity to raise enough cash to acquire
otherwise inaccessible land. Unfortunately, things have rarely
turned out this way in practice. Instead, no sooner is money
collected for the purchase of land, than that money — and the
land — is as good as gone. In some cases the very politicians who
organized the companies and initiated the collection of money
then used company funds to buy the land privately: there has been
little that their powerless victims could do to intervene. A recent
example of this sort of manoeuvre involves a former cabinet
minister from Kisii. During his days of political glory he deliberately
organized two rival companies, Gesarate Farmers Ltd. and Nyaribari
Farmers Co-operative Society, in order to buy a 2,385 acre farm
in Trans-Nzoia. A little later, the by now ex-minister, who was
acting as the second company's lawyer, turned around and sued the
first company which he himself had formed. Irregularities in the
registration of Nyaribari Farmers' Co-operative Society (the

directors are members of his immediate family) suggest that the ex-minister wants to acquire the farm himself. Shs. 5 million, exclusive of interest, is likely to be lost by the farmers concerned.

Cheating the landless has become a lucrative way of life for Kenya's *waBenzi*. In Central Province alone at least 250 land companies had sprung up by 1975, generally under the leadership of local politicians or important businessmen. The P.C. reported that most of them were 'in a total mess'. In Nyeri District alone 60 such companies owed their members a total of shs. 50 million in 1981, and 26 were nearly bankrupt. In Kiambu District such land companies as the Mbo-i-Kamiti Farmers' Company pose a scandal of unusual dimensions. In the mid-1970s a minister of state used Presidential Prerogative to acquire half a dozen or more large coffee estates and then sold 'shares' of the land to more than 3,000 peasant farmers. Unfortunately for the farmers, no one seems to know what happened to the share capital or who actually owns the land. Neither dividends nor coffee returns have been given to the duped 'shareholders'. The P.C. of Central Province meanwhile reports that about 50,000 families have been cheated of at least shs. 100 million according to his records. The figure is much higher if interest for 15 years is computed. Of course, many bogus companies are not registered, but simply disappear overnight after selling 'shares'.

In Nakuru, Ndeffo (Nakuru District Ex-Freedom Fighters Organisation), Ngwataniro, and Wanyororo companies were declared insolvent and are now under 'investigation'; 60,000 families are affected. Ngwataniro alone has shs. 50 million share capital and assets worth shs. 120 million. It has never audited its accounts, and has no regular annual general meeting. It was recently estimated that shs. 54 million had been embezzled by officials of the company. In order to gain some protection a group of Ndeffo members have, by sheer defiance, forced the government to sanction the sub-division of their farms. The other members of the three companies have had to content themselves with frequent promises of future prosperity made by already prosperous company directors.

Thanks to widespread property racketeering, the land issue threatens to become as explosive in 'independent' Kenya as it was during the colonial period. Parliament from time to time makes a brave attempt to discuss the issue. Private motions have been brought by members requesting the government to revise the terms of tenure, or put a ceiling on land prices and the amount of land which can be held by a single individual. Questions have been raised concerning the enormous amount of land in foreign hands, and the idle land held for merely speculative purposes. The government's response is always the same. Behind the scenes the M.P.s who dare ask such questions are threatened, their potential supporters intimidated, while the 'willing seller willing buyer' formula is trotted out for public consumption. How long will these 'willing buyers' and grabbers be free to trample over our land and our people?

Appendix 6

Who's Co-operating Here?

Farmers' co-operatives were started by and for the colonial settlers more than 50 years ago to provide them with a marketing infra-structure. They were extended to African small producers in the 1950s as an instrument of 'quality control' and way of stimulating the cash-crop economy in the 'reserves'. Up until the mid-1960s this strategy was remarkably successful. Because it was mandatory to be a member of a co-operative society in order to grow or sell a given cash-crop, African producers in all regions joined divisional co-operative societies to market their coffee, tea, pyrethrum, sugar, and cotton, as well as other farm produce such as pork, dairy and poultry products. These divisional societies were then joined together into larger bureaucratic 'District Co-operative Unions' designed to oversee the running of the divisional societies. Practically all districts in the agricultural regions of Kenya have these 'District Unions'.

Since the mid-1960s matters have taken a drastic turn for the worse as far as members of the co-operatives are concerned. They have repeatedly found themselves the victims of mismanagement, embezzling and other corrupt practices carried out by society and union officials, generally with the complicity and protection of the politicians and government agents. The result has been not only huge losses for the farmers concerned, but also a decline in rural production and income. Given the extent to which the co-operative movement has betrayed their interests, it is hardly surprising that large numbers of farmers have begun to pull out of the societies.

The failure of the co-operative movement is vividly illustrated by developments in the region around Mt. Kenya (including Murang'a and Kiambu). In this area, coffee co-operatives have specialized in the theft of farmers' earnings. For instance, in Meru, a publicly-reported shs. 72 million went missing between 1978 and 1980, while in Kiambu and Kirinyaga respectively shs. 68 million and 72 million have similarly been lost, largely through embezzlement and faulty investments in the last three years. Similarly, in Murang'a District, the Mugoiri Coffee Co-operative Society has an undetermined large sum unaccounted for. This has meant that farmers have not been paid for deliveries for well over a year. In fact, in 1980 and 1981 payments to farmers have been either minimal or non-existent in the entire region. In January 1981 the societies, with the explicit approval of the Ministry of Co-operative Development, issued IOU circulars to be presented to schools in lieu of school fees! This situation was due both to co-operative mismanagement and the general foreign exchange crisis. In an attempt to cope with this crisis, the government has 'borrowed', interest-free, farmers' earnings for use elsewhere in the economy. Members have retaliated by fighting co-operative officials and police in both Murang'a and Kiambu. In early 1981, Weithaga farmers barricaded the roads leading to factories and chased away police and district administrators.

But by far the most glaring example of inefficiency, theft, and destruction of rural productivity is that of the various Nyeri District coffee and dairy co-operative societies including the umbrella Nyeri District Co-operative Union. The divisional Tetu Coffee Growers Co-operative Society owed farmers a reported shs. 3 million for 1979 alone. In protest, farmers stopped coffee harvesting and delivery to factories until government set up a probe commission which revealed that an additional shs. 6 million had disappeared. The Mukurweini Coffee Growers Co-operative Society has lost more than shs. 80 million between 1977 and 1980. Of this, a staggering shs. 54 million vanished in the single year of 1978 through a complicated system of theft-accounting and bogus property deals involving the local M.P. (then assistant minister in the Office of the President). A damning report by the Provincial Co-operatives officer was hushed and the officer himself transferred. The Ministry for Co-operative Development subsequently carried out a probe whose results were curtly announced by the Minister in early 1980: 'no corruption found'. In this case, the *known* sum of money unaccounted for means a loss of some shs.3,000 per coffee farmer per year within that period. It must be pointed out again that these figures represent only auditable items, and do not cover such 'invisible' losses as those due to underweighing produce, and overpayment for goods and services.

The net effect of this corruption and incompetence is a drastic drop in co-operative society membership, and a turning toward informal individual marketing channels or away altogether from the cash-crop economy. Thus, the Mukurweini Dairy Co-operative Society has been wound up after farmers stopped milk deliveries. In Mathira, dairy co-operative membership has dropped from approximately 12,000 in 1977 to 2,000 in 1981, and the society is about to wind up operations. In the meantime, Kenya, previously a net exporter, has to import dairy products from Europe and suffers endemic milk shortages. (See Appendix 7.)

The Mt. Kenya region is not unique for co-operative mismanagement. Similar cases can be cited from other farming areas of the country. Non-farming co-operatives are also often poorly managed. For example, the Kenya Union of Savings and Credit Co-operatives, which represents many savings co-operatives all over Kenya, with a membership of almost 500,000, was reported by external auditors to have huge financial irregularities involving several million shillings. Among other things, the Union had no official voucher system, and no inventory of assets, while the budgets generally were not approved by relevant bodies. Foreign donor agencies were angered when a probe team appointed by the Commissioner of Co-operatives was suddenly called off by the Ministry in order to protect high-level union thieves. Meanwhile, low-level thieves from local savings co-operatives continue to make the news one day and be absolved the next.

Appendix 7

Feeding the Plutocrats: The Parastatals

Key sectors of the Kenyan economy are at present mismanaged by more than 50 vaguely-defined quasi-government organizations, statutory boards and parastatals. The parastatal wingspan has spread to cover many aspects of agricultural production, finance, industry, commerce, transport and services. Most parastatals are economic disasters. Despite generous government protection, and massive public financial support, only the occasional one ever returns a profit to the Treasury. Most verge on bankruptcy. To avoid detection they delay issuing annual reports for up to five years as one minister recently observed while castigating the National Irrigation Board as a 'sick baby'. The managers of these organizations do not seem to consider chronic inefficiency a problem. In fact, they do not seem to be concerned with much besides their own stomachs. The parastatals provide them with permanent banqueting halls. And when they have eaten their way through one particular menu and want to taste new delights, they can be shifted to other parastatal eating areas. Trying to sort out who is doing what where is like trying to sort out cooked spaghetti. Utter confusion prevails in the parastatals, as the chairman of one body today is rewarded for his abuse of office by being made the chairman of another body tomorrow. The very vagueness of the parastatals — their amorphous outlines and spheres of operation — make them ideal eating places. Whenever there are too few seats at the table, whenever it seems as if some well-connected plutocrat might have to go without his supper, a new parastatal can be created and given him to preside over, as was recently done in the case of the Kerio Valley Development Authority. As far as the parastatal bodies are concerned, the needs of the officials predominate; the needs of the country come a poor second, if they are considered at all.

To be more specific, let us look at the examples of the Kenya Meat Commission (KMC), Kenya Co-operative Creameries (KCC), and the former Wheat Board (now part of National Cereals and Produce Board, a body recently created to give the appearance of a 'new start' when the old Maize and Produce Board and Wheat Board foundered so badly). Before 1970 KMC and KCC were fairly successful commercial concerns enjoying their colonial legacy of monopoly rights over meat and dairy production. During the last decade, however, the health of these bodies has been drastically impaired, at enormous cost to the economy, taxpayer, and the producers of the commodities concerned. KMC alone has averaged shs. 15 million annually in direct state subsidies. Despite these subsidies, its expanded internal market and large export outlets, it is always on the brink of bankruptcy. In 1978, the Minister of Agriculture reported that KMC had received shs. 56 million in direct aid that year, as well as a government loan guarantee to commercial banks. Why then was the KMC in such drastic straits? Its new managing director hotly denied any mismanagement, and shifted the blame on to past managers. He failed to mention that his previous job — that of chief executive of the pig industry parastatal — had ended in similar chaos. Instead, he chose to see his transfer to KMC as a promotion by the government since he had done such a spectacular job disorganizing the Uplands Bacon factory.

But perhaps he was no worse than his KMC predecessor: quality and responsibility in management are two attributes which most parastatal directors scorn. That predecessor, who subsequently hopped over to a newly created parastatal, Kenya Airways, had set a high standard for thievery. He served as an agent of the ruling Family which had been eyeing the meat business as a possible area of grabbing, especially the recently discovered Middle East market. Procedures were hastily set in motion to establish an 'export abattoir' in competition with KMC. Halal Meat Products Ltd. was born, endowed with public land, a shs. 30 million interest-free government loan (channelled from Danish aid and government sources), and government-paid veterinary officers. According to a ministerial statement in Parliament, the 'big fish' were behind the entire project, but they used a small-time meat dealer and his wife as front-men for the company. As it turned out, the real mover behind the company was KMC management. Halal went into liquidation in 1981 and was declared bankrupt, having served its purpose as a conduit for public funds. It is estimated that shs. 100 million, excluding the 20 acres of land at Ngong, was annexed in this manner. The government characteristically ignored the whole proceedings, and continued its annual subsidies to KMC. Meanwhile illegal meat exports — most recently carried out by the big brass in the armed forces — are stepped up, despite chronic meat shortages in the internal market. Farmers have boycotted KMC due to low prices and delayed payments. The abattoir at Mombasa has been closed for 'lack of animals for slaughter'. To give the appearance of some kind of action on the deteriorating meat front, the President has appointed a new boss to lead KMC, and rewarded the old one with a lateral shift to a different parastatal.

A similar dismal story can be told of KCC, which has a virtual monopoly over dairy production. In the last decade, Kenya has been reduced from a major exporter of dairy products to a net importer, thanks largely to KCC's discouragement of farmers and disorganization of the dairy infrastructure. At the same time as annual dry season milk shortages are partly alleviated by imports of powdered milk, the few farmers who continue in the dairy business complain about poor milk collection and payment by KCC. While KCC faces insolvency, and the government comes annually to its financial rescue, the usual top management fiddles go on, concerning vehicles, agricultural machinery and general misuse of funds.

As for food grains, they have until recently been at the mercy of the Wheat Board and the National Maize and Produce Board, both now incorporated into a new National Cereals and Produce Board formed to induce the public to forget the past. The Maize Board, on behalf of the Ministry of Agriculture, had in the last few years presided over growing hunger in Kenya. The then head of the board (an ex-P.C. of Nairobi) has received a fitting prize for his stirling performance in the maize-smuggling saga — again as if to induce the public to forget the past, he has changed his name and been made head of the largest industrial parastatal. The old Wheat Board, like its sister in maize production, had managed to preside over the decline of wheat growing from a peak of almost 250,000 tons in the late 1960s to a mere 150,000 tons in 1980, forcing Kenya to become a net importer of wheat. Meanwhile, the board was in debt to the tune of a reported shs. 46 million. Danish loans totalling shs. 124 million have been squandered in the construction of three over-priced, possibly sub-standard storage silos in Rift Valley Province, while expensive machinery sits rusting at Mombasa. The cost to the people of Kenya is heavy in terms of loan and interest repayments and expensive wheat import bills. The new Cereals Board seems to have taken up where the old Wheat Board left off — grain imports will have to continue if Kenyans are to have bread.

The above three parastatals — KMC, KCC and the Cereals Board — deal with agricultural produce. Their performance is matched by parastatals in the 'service' sector, such as those which were created after the collapse of the East African Community: the Harbours Corporation, Kenya Airways, and Kenya Railways. These parastatals were formed by politicians and businessmen who had a financial stake in destroying the Community. A glance at subsequent mismanagement of the Railways shows a familiar picture of corruption and ineptitude. The Railways served as a feeding zone for an influential ex-minister Bruce Mackenzie, and his close friends in the cabinet. The 'Mackenzie boys' engineered the overturning of a contract originally awarded to a Canadian company, and, with a little help from the British High Commissioner handed it over to a British supplier instead. Benefits reaped by the Mackenzie crowd were probably in excess of the reported £30 million. The Kenya Railways Corporation has since then seldom been free of scandal and financial crisis.

The examples cited above of parastatal plundering of the economy can be multiplied many times. In practically all cases, parastatals have been inefficient at management but quite efficient at siphoning off surplus for the directors and their politician friends. In spite of their notoriety, in no case has a serious probe of parastatal performance ever been undertaken, either by government or by the toothless Inspectorate of Statutory Bodies. The high level KMC and KCC investigations of 1978 and 1979 were killed when prominent political figures intervened. Where low level probes have been attempted, reports have generally been suppressed, since they incriminate influential members of the ruling class. Employees of parastatal organizations have even recently had their pay scales boosted! It seems that the parastatal feeding grounds are probably safe for future 'eating', as long as the country can endure them.

Appendix 8

Food Games

Despite four consecutive good maize harvests and one record bumper crop in 1978, Kenyans had no staple food of their own in 1980–81, and had to depend on the outside for grains. Long queues and food riots were common in town and country. There was widespread starvation, especially in the north. How can this be explained?

Kenya's marketable maize averages about 5 million bags a year. In 1978, after several years of above-average maize crops, the country had a massive harvest of more than 10 million bags, and was in a position to replenish future strategic reserves and even export some maize. What happened to this harvest has never been explained. All of it, *including* the strategic reserves of 5.5 million bags, was either exported at a net loss to the government and taxpayer, or smuggled out of the country at considerable gain to someone. The country had to import or starve. Certain things are clear: maize racketeering had been going on since 1976 at least. Between 1978 and 1979 a clique of ministers used their closeness to the centre of power to export the strategic maize reserves, and while they were at it obtained sole grain import rights. In 1979,

with the country's reserves nearly depleted, the Minister for
Agriculture authorized a UN World Food Programme swop of
8,110 tons of Canadian Wheat for 12,000 tons of Kenyan maize
(to be used for Zambian relief). The disappearance of our food
must be attributed to criminal corruption plus incompetence.

Despite frequent questions raised in Parliament, and tantalizing
contradictory statements issued by successive Ministers of
Agriculture, the government has refused to investigate what
happened to the food supply. Cabinet quibbling over maize
became a national scandal, with one minister — who should know
what he was talking about — claiming that the 'big people' were
smuggling food, and that what was needed was 'an injection of
public morality into the country's political leadership'. One M.P.
wondered if there was a 'Mafia-type group operating in the country
which was stronger than the government.' Instead of addressing
itself to the issue, the government engaged in a high-level cover-up,
and got out its begging bowl. By early 1980 the President had
obtained food loans to the tune of an initial $30 million from the
U.S. but was less successful elsewhere. According to the then
Minister of Agriculture, shs. 540 million were spent to buy maize
and wheat and rice from countries like the U.S., Australia, and
South Africa. The imported 200,000 tons of grain did not, however,
put an end to these disastrous food games. At the height of the
shortages a ministerial co-ordinating committee in the Office of
the President hotly disputed middleman rights. Much to the disgust
of the USAID officials, some U.S. shipments had apparently been
re-exported by ministerial middlemen, or declared 'substandard'
and sold elsewhere. The failure of our people to secure adequate
supplies after the shipments had arrived and presumably been
distributed was blamed by government on hoarding by kiosk
owners, and on an anti-government conspiracy!

Smuggling, corruption and drought tell part of the shortage
story; poor government planning for storage, the lack of a coherent
food policy and incentives to the producers, and punitive quality
controls tell the rest. The grandiose Sessional Paper No. 4 for 1981,
a belated attempt to come to terms with the food disaster,
promises to be as unworkable as the development plans which
preceded it. Given the maize muddle, it is hardly surprising that
farmers are turning away from food grain production to other
crops, such as malt barley much in demand by the Breweries. At
this rate, our people will be hungry tomorrow, but after spending
the day on line outside the *duka* they will be able to console

themselves with a Tusker (bottled beer).

Appendix 9

The University Meal-Ticket

The thousands of students who come to Nairobi to take up their studies arrive with high hopes. They will learn more than they had bargained for. They will learn that, in addition to courses, the University offers a reflection of the looting and mismanagement taking place at all levels of society, and that the administration and government as often as not regarded the academic staff and students with open hostility.

There is no communication between the two sides, and no sense of common purpose. One side is dedicated to preserving the University as an arena for 'eating'; the other side concerned to maintain some semblance of academic standards. The advantage lies with the administration, which is linked directly to the government through its Chancellor and government-appointed Council. The Council itself is composed of big businessmen and politicians with little tolerance for academic debate. Neither do they respect procedural regularity. University decisions are taken independently of the various institutional organs specified in the 1970 University Act. Impromptu closures and openings as often as not originate in State House where the Chancellor resides.

The custom of closing down the University whenever conflict threatened began in 1969, and became the routine way of dealing with problems from the mid-1970s. In the last few years there have been approximately two major closures a year, some lasting several months. The students might find themselves suddenly sent home 'to participate in elections' or for an 'early Christmas holiday' or 'early Easter'. Student unrest is invariably blamed on the weather, or on foreign ideologies or disgruntled politicians, or outside agitators. Student organizations which have attempted to articulate grievances have been banned altogether or replaced with puppet bodies. The administration does not want to hear what the students have to say because it cannot afford to. Students and staff demand a thorough examination of the way the University functions, and thorough-going reforms. The governing body is intent on covering up its misdeeds, and continuing its old ways. If the University falls apart in the process, that is not its concern.

A full expose of criminal mismanagement at the University would contain some spectacular findings. After a recent student riot in the dining hall, the tip (of the tip) of the iceberg was publicly revealed. It appears that catering has long been Big Business. For years everyone had known that University food was supplied exclusively by one Chancellor with extensive farms near Nairobi. It subsequently came to light that dining hall supervisors and janitors had set up a ring to sell off University food to city workers. Other administrators got into the act, and students were fed horsemeat and wildlife while the food intended for them was sold elsewhere at a handsome profit. A little bit of digging revealed that there were 300 'ghost' cooks on the payroll — all from the same village! At this point the digging was hastily abandoned, the manager of the Central Catering Unit sent on 'leave', and that was an end to the saga as far as the public was concerned. Around the same time, the major thieves at Kenyatta University College were transferred to handsome positions in the Ministry of Education. Back at the University, it was business as usual, which meant that the usual rip-offs continued.

The lucrative areas outside the food trade are the housing racket, the construction business, and the practice of stealing from University stores. The University has refused to build staff housing on land provided for that purpose. Instead, it houses its staff in various expensive suburbs, and spends over one million shillings a month paying landlords rent at a higher rate than the market value. The landlords in question turn out to be politicians, civil servants and University councillors. The University also pays shs. 150,000 a month or so for shoddy furniture from a company which has a monopoly of the University trade and close connections with the Council. While the Council deals in real estate (one University 'landlord' gets shs. 91,000 a month from the institution), the students are crammed into dorms, or booked into cheap hotels. There are 8-10 in a room in condemned housing at Kenyatta University College, living in circumstances which make study nearly impossible. Conditions are not likely to improve in the future, since the construction business is another major area of administrative 'eating'. There have been several known cases of collusion between the administration and contractors. On some campuses funds designated for new buildings have been diverted into individual pockets, with the result that the buildings themselves are substandard and only half-finished. Needless to say, there have

been no official inquiries, or attempts to account for the seepage
of funds. The same general lack of accountability afflicts the
University stores. Stealing supplies is child's play, since the managers
of the stores apparently do not recognize the value of record-
keeping and simply have no idea what is coming or going. Lately,
it appears that less has been coming and more going — who knows
where? Lecturers have been forced to supply their own chalk and
erasers. The flair for mismanagement which characterizes the catering
unit and the University stores, is also evident in the running of the
University veterinarian and coffee farms, the Correspondence
Course Unit, bookshop, computer centre, and halls of residence.
In all these University undertakings there seems to be a positive
aversion toward keeping reliable books, and the idea of individual
and collective responsibility.

Meanwhile, the University is facing bankruptcy. It owes millions
to creditors. It is presently unable to budget its month to month
running costs, and has had to rob workers' pension funds, savings
co-operatives and research funds in order to keep the place going.
It is now shut yet again 'indefinitely'. For months the government
had been looking for an excuse to close down the institution for
nine months, in order to balance the budget, and, more importantly,
to shift the academic year so that on 2 March (JM Day) students
would be dispersed. In May, authorities got the excuse they had
been looking for when the students, in one of their most protracted
struggles to date, went into the streets in defiance of government
and G.S.U. They were expressing solidarity with government
doctors who had similarly defied the government and gone on a
prolonged strike. They were also opposing administrative tyranny
and KANU chicanery in Bondo and Busia. The government has
reacted like a wounded buffalo, victimizing students and staff,
and taking desperate illegal measures against them. The students
are now either in hospital, jail, or under 'village arrest' in the
custody of their chiefs. Meanwhile the plans for a second
university continue.

OTHER BOOKS AVAILABLE FROM ZED

On Africa
A. Temu and B. Swai
Historians and Africanist History
A Critique
Hb and Pb

Dan Nabudere
Imperialism in East Africa: Vols. I & II
Hb

Horst Drechsler
Let us Die Fighting
Namibia under the Germans
Hb and Pb

Chris Searle
We're Building the New School
Diary of a Teacher in Mozambique
Hb

Okwudiba Nnoli (Ed.)
Path to Nigerian Development
Pb

Robert Archer and Antoine Bouillon
The South African Game
Sport and Racism in South Africa
Hb and Pb

SWAPO Department of Information and Publicity
To Be Born a Nation
The Liberation Struggle for Namibia
Pb

Ben Turok (Ed.)
Development in Zambia
A Reader
Pb

Edwin Madunagu
Problems of Socialism
The Nigerian Challenge
Pb

Claude Ake
Revolutionary Pressures in Africa
Hb and Pb

Baruch Hirson
Year of Fire, Year of Ash
The Soweto Revolt: Roots of a Revolution?
Hb and Pb

Maina wa Kinyatti
Thunder from the Mountains
Mau Mau Patriotic Songs
Hb

No Sizwe
One Azania, One Nation
The National Question in South Africa
Hb and Pb

Albert Nzula and others
Forced Labour in Colonial Africa
Hb and Pb

Justinian Rweyemamu (ed.)
Industrialization and Income Distribution in Africa
Hb and Pb

Ann Seidman and Neva Makgetla
Outposts of Monopoly Capitalism
Southern Africa in the Changing Global Economy
Pb

Elenga M'buyinga
Pan Africanism or Neo-colonialism
The Bankruptcy of the OAU
Hb and Pb

Faarax Cawl
Ignorance is the Enemy of Love
Pb

Mohamed Babu
African Socialism or Socialist Africa?
Hb and Pb

Aquino de Braganca and Immanuel Wallerstein (Eds)
The African Liberation Reader
Documents of the National Liberation Movements (3 vols.)
Hb

Basil Davidson
No Fist is Big Enough to Hide the Sky
The Liberation of Guinea and Cape Verde: Aspects of an African Revolution
Hb

Eduardo Mondlane
The Struggle for Mozambique
Hb and Pb

Yolamu Barongo (Ed.)
Political Science in Africa
A Radical Critique
Hb and Pb

Bade Onimode
Imperialism and Underdevelopment in Nigeria
The Dialectics of Poverty
Hb and Pb

Ronald Graham
The Aluminium Industry and the Third World
Hb and Pb

Henrik Marcussen and Jens Torp
The Internationalization of Capital: The Prospects for the Third World
A Re-examination of Dependency Theory
Hb and Pb

Louis Wolf and others (Eds.)
Dirty Work: The CIA in Africa
Hb and Pb

Peder Gouwenius
Power to the People
South Africa in Struggle: A Pictorial History
Pb

Zed Press titles cover Africa, Asia, Latin America and the Middle East, as well as general issues affecting the Third World's relations with the rest of the world. Our Series embrace: Imperialism, Women, Political Economy, History, Labour, Voices of Struggle, Human Rights and other areas pertinent to the Third World.

You can order Zed titles direct from Zed Press, 57 Caledonian Road, London, N1 9DN, U.K.

Why the Journal for African Marxists?

Objectives

1. To provide a **forum** for the exposition of the fundamentals of Marxism in the conditions of Africa;
2. To encourage thoroughgoing **analysis** of the problems of development in Africa from a Marxist perspective;
3. To discuss the various versions of socialism current in Africa and subject them to scientific and constructive **criticism**;
4. To facilitate the emergence of a systematic and coherent Marxist **body of thought** illuminating conditions in Africa;
5. To serve as an **instrument** for the creation of Marxist discussion groups which shall develop alternative policies for Africa based on Scientific Socialism.

Background

This independent initiative aims to set up a continent-wide forum in which African scholars and activists will try to facilitate the emergence of a systematic and coherent body of Marxist thought illuminating conditions in Africa and generating support for people's struggles against imperialism and for scientific socialism. The Provisional Editorial Board is in Zambia and local committees already exist in Ghana, Lesotho, Nigeria, Swaziland, Tanzania, Zimbabwe, Paris and London.

Issue 1 (November 1981) contained articles by Mohamed Babu of Tanzania, Elenga M'buyinga, Vice-President of Manidem the Cameroonian opposition front; Professor Bernard Magubane, the South African sociologist; and Dr. Bonaventure Swai, the Tanzanian historian.

Issue 2 (August 1982) included articles by Professor Emmanuel Hansen on Ghana since the Rawlings coup; Dr. Mpakathi, President of Lesoma, the Socialist League of Malawi etc.

Subscriptions

	Africa	U.K.	Elsewhere
Individuals	£4.00	£4.00	£5.00
Institutions	£6.00	£7.00	£9.00

For airmail subscription, add £3.00.

Subscriptions to the *Journal of African Marxists*, 57 Caledonian Road, London N1 9DN.

Single copy orders to Zed Press.